Creating Effective
TEAMS

FOURTH EDITION

Creating Effective TEAMS

A Guide for Members and Leaders

FOURTH EDITION

Susan A. Wheelan

GDQ Associates, Inc.

Los Angeles | London | New Delhi
Singapore | Washington DC

Los Angeles | London | New Delhi
Singapore | Washington DC

FOR INFORMATION:

SAGE Publications, Inc.
2455 Teller Road
Thousand Oaks, California 91320
E-mail: order@sagepub.com

SAGE Publications Ltd.
1 Oliver's Yard
55 City Road
London EC1Y 1SP
United Kingdom

SAGE Publications India Pvt. Ltd.
B 1/I 1 Mohan Cooperative Industrial Area
Mathura Road, New Delhi 110 044
India

SAGE Publications Asia-Pacific Pte. Ltd.
3 Church Street
#10-04 Samsung Hub
Singapore 049483

Acquisitions Editor: Patricia Quinlin
Editorial Assistant: Katie Guarino
Production Editor: Libby Larson
Copy Editor: Rachel Keith
Typesetter: C&M Digitals (P) Ltd.
Proofreader: Susan Schon
Indexer: Molly Hall
Cover Designer: Anupama Krishnan
Marketing Manager: Liz Thornton
Permissions Editor: Karen Ehrmann

Copyright © 2013 by SAGE Publications, Inc.

Printed in the United States of America

Library of Congress Cataloging-in-Publication Data

Wheelan, Susan A.
Creating effective teams: a guide for members and leaders/Susan A. Wheelan.—4th ed.

p. cm.
Includes bibliographical references and index.

ISBN 978-1-4522-1707-9 (pbk.)

1. Teams in the workplace. I. Title.

HD66.W485 2013
658.4′022—dc23   2012001311

This book is printed on acid-free paper.

13 14 15 16 10 9 8 7 6 5 4 3 2

BRIEF CONTENTS

DETAILED CONTENTS

ACKNOWLEDGMENTS

SAGE Publications would like to thank the following reviewers:

Barbara Barton
Western Michigan University

David Biemer
Texas State University

David Conrad, Ed.D.
Augsburg College

Elise Freed-Fagan, Ph.D.
Community College of Philadelphia

Meghan O. Gill
Kean University

Dr. Mahesh S. Raisinghani
TWU School of Management

⋈ ONE ⋈

WHY GROUPS?

Groups Have a Long History of Success

People have formed work groups to accomplish goals and tasks since the beginning of human history. The small group, whose members work collaboratively for their mutual benefit or survival, is the oldest form of social organization. Groups have played a major role in both the survival of human beings and the development of human culture. Some would argue that our ability to work together was, and is, the key to human survival and advancement. Work groups have a long and remarkable track record of success. From the beginning of human history, people have utilized work groups to generate new ideas, get things done, and nurture individuals.

We Need Groups Every Day

The vast majority of people participate in work groups on a daily basis and have always done so. Imagine building a house or an airplane, putting out a newspaper, developing a strategic plan, or doing almost anything, all by yourself. Of course, there are tasks that can, or should, be done by one person, but given the complex nature of work in the 21st century, more and more tasks require people to work in groups.

There was a time when people tried to get rid of the collaborative nature of work. We set up assembly lines and precisely defined each person's job so that he or she could do that job without input from others. Often, this was effective. The industrial revolution was a success, after all. But this strategy worked best for repetitive tasks where innovation, creativity, and problem solving were not necessary. In the 21st century, humans perform few tasks like that. Most of those jobs are left to robots.

Even during the early industrial period there were groups throughout the workplace. People made decisions together. Engineers created new products together. Managers determined schedules and hammered out work flow processes together. There was a need for work groups then, and there is an even greater need for work groups now.

Groups Increase Our Knowledge Base

Work groups reflect our growing awareness that the complexity of work at this point in history requires collaboration. More work is conducted by groups of employees than by individuals because collaboration is the only way to accomplish complex tasks. Too much knowledge and too many different skills are required for any individual to accomplish such tasks successfully alone.

The knowledge explosion led us to reevaluate the way we work. The assembly line model has lost much of its relevance. The individual contributor no longer can go it alone. Teamwork is necessary for organizational success.

When Teams Are Good, They're Very, Very Good

Lots of people don't like to work in groups. Many of us think meetings are a waste of time. Most of us have had bad experiences working in groups. Some of us associate work groups with fighting, hurt feelings, and inefficiency. This is not surprising, since many groups have difficulty functioning effectively. Even groups that ultimately succeed in becoming teams have periods that are stressful and unpleasant.

The distinction between a work group and a team is an important one in this book. A work group is composed of members who are striving to create a shared view of goals and to develop an efficient and effective organizational structure in which to accomplish those goals. A work group becomes a team when shared goals have been established and effective methods to accomplish those goals are in place. How work groups become teams is what this book is about. It chronicles how some groups develop into high performance teams and why other groups fail to become teams. Throughout the book, I refer to groups that have not reached a level of effectiveness and productivity as *work groups* and to groups that are effective and productive as *teams*.

When a group becomes a team, there is nothing like it. Work doesn't feel like a chore. It's fun. Members of high performance teams feel involved, committed, and valued. Time flies, work flows, and people help each other to meet goals and deadlines. There's nothing like playing on a winning team. Effective teams are more productive, and that means that companies and organizations win, too. The trick to creating teams is to learn enough about how work groups function so that we can increase the chances that work groups will become high performance teams.

Creating Effective Teams

Books, articles, and research studies that attempt to describe the characteristics of high performance work teams proliferated for some time. The importance of teamwork in increasing organizational productivity was clear, and everyone jumped on the bandwagon to ensure team success. Employees and leaders went to training sessions to learn how to work in teams. In some companies, employees wore T-shirts with their team name printed on the front. Teams often were provided with leaders, coaches, facilitators, or consultants. The intense focus on teams and team performance made teamwork seem new and faddish, even though working together to get things done is as old as humanity itself.

BOX 1.1   Silly Team-Building Activities

Over the years, I've asked people to describe the silliest team-building activity they've participated in. Here are some of my favorites:

- Introductions involving linking your name with a personality trait (e.g., Chatty Cathy, Serious Sam, Jumpy Jill)
- Racing dragon boats as a team to sell more insurance policies
- Leading a blindfolded teammate along the beach
- Anything involving sharing feelings you don't want to share
- Anything that requires rope (such as rock climbing or rope bridges)
- Anything requiring construction paper

While "teaming" may have felt like a fad or a craze, it wasn't. Groups and teams have always been with us and won't go away. The importance of teams in the workplace is here to stay. However, there is limited awareness of how work groups function and how members and leaders can work together to create effective and productive teams.

Unfortunately, in the current decade, the focus on work groups has dramatically decreased. Instead of educating work groups, consisting of members and their leader, attention has shifted to educating team leaders. It is assumed that knowledgeable team leaders will be able to steer their groups to high performance and productivity. Between 1990 and 2000, 172 research studies of work groups and 54 studies of team leadership were carried out. Between 2000 and 2010, only 78 research studies of work groups and teams were done. During the same period, there were 126 studies of work group leadership.

This change in focus—from how group members and their leader work together to how the leader steers the group—seems to represent unrealistic expectations. If members don't know about or understand the dynamics of groups and group development, it will be very difficult for their work group to become a high performance team. Members and leaders need knowledge and skills if their work group is to be productive.

Which strategies help work group members and their leader? Which strategies are based on solid research evidence? Which strategies are least time consuming and most cost effective? These and similar questions are on the minds of many people charged with ensuring the effectiveness of organizational work groups. The good news is that the scientific study of work groups and high performance teams has made the answers to these questions easier to come by.

We don't yet know everything there is to know about groups, but we know enough to assist people working in groups. We know enough to answer the difficult questions posed earlier. That's what this book is about. The goal of *Creating Effective Teams* is to translate what we've learned about groups and teams into straightforward, user-friendly, practical guidelines for members and leaders. This book will also provide guidance for those who interact with a particular work group and for those who manage them.

I bring about 40 years of experience with groups and teams to this project, and I'm not bored yet. Studying groups and working with their members is endlessly fascinating and challenging. Beyond that, I believe that helping work groups to become high performance teams is crucial not only to the bottom line but also to the creation of humane, interesting, diverse, and challenging workplaces. I hope this book continues the work of the first three editions in furthering the achievement of those goals.

How to Use This Book

Originally, this book grew out of a number of requests I'd had from organizational members to write a jargon-free "how-to" book describing how work groups function and what to do to help work groups become high performance teams. While I was not enamored of how-to books, I decided to try my hand at this one because the topic is so important. My decision turned out to be a good one. *Creating Effective Teams* has been read by thousands of team members and leaders, in a number of countries, as well as by team consultants charged with helping groups to become high performance teams. I wrote this fourth edition to keep the ball rolling and to add new information that has emerged since the third edition was published.

As in the first three editions, whatever I write will be based on research evidence, and if I'm speculating, I'll let you know. I promise not to overwhelm you with references in the text; those references will appear at the end of the book. If you want more information, the references will be there for you. In fact, in response to requests from readers, I have included more references and recent studies.

I've included recent research throughout the book and a few things I've heard, witnessed, been told about, or asked people about over the years. These will appear in boxes like the one in this chapter. These anecdotes have helped me, as well as people I've worked with, to maintain a sense of humor and compassion about working in groups and teams. I hope you find them useful.

This book is meant to be used, not just read. Members of newly formed groups can get off to a good start by reading the first six chapters and discussing them together. Chapter 2 describes how groups develop and function. Chapters 3 to 6 describe what group members and their leader can do to help move the group through the stages of group development. Chapter 7 describes how high performance teams function. Chapter 8 outlines how team members can contribute to a work group's development and effectiveness. Chapter 9 describes how to be an effective team leader. Finally, Chapter 10 discusses the importance of organizational support for teams.

Talk with each other about what you've read. Use the information as a way to begin to organize your group. Refer to the book as you would a manual for a computer program. When you get stuck, find the appropriate chapter. Use the checklists scattered throughout the book to monitor your group's progress.

Once the group gets under way, refer to Chapter 3, which describes situations that often arise in the first stage of group development and outlines ways that members and leaders can be helpful during this stage. Chapters 4 and 5 do the same for groups at Stages 2 and 3, respectively. Chapter 6 outlines how to reach and sustain high performance at Stage 4.

Learning to implement this information in the work groups you belong to will take time, and reading this book once won't be enough. Attitudes and behaviors don't change overnight. If you read and work with the information, however, it will happen. And you, like others before you, will find your work groups transformed into high performance teams.

TWO

FROM GROUPS TO TEAMS

The Stages of Group Development

———◆———

Groups develop across time very much like people do. People experience childhood, adolescence, young adulthood, adulthood, and old age. Childhood is associated with dependency. Adolescence usually contains some periods of conflict. Young adulthood requires that people spend a lot of time developing trusting relationships and preparing for work careers. In adulthood people spend a significant amount of time working, and in old age people typically reduce their focus on work. Research has found that groups also experience periods of dependency, conflict, trust and structuring, work, and disengagement. Group development and human development have much in common.

The concept of group development is well documented in the social science literature. In view of the general consensus that groups develop and change across time, extensive reviews of the literature have been conducted to consolidate previous research and to propose a unified model of group development. These reviews have produced similar results. What follows is a brief description of the integrated model of group development that I use in my own work. This model was initially based on previous research. Since then, a number of studies have been conducted to determine whether these stages actually occur in work groups. To date, these studies have confirmed that the stages of development outlined in the model do occur in groups in the real world.

The overall goal of group development is to create an organized unit capable of working effectively and productively to achieve specific ends. The goals of each stage are outlined in the next four sections.

Stage 1: Dependency and Inclusion

Goals of Stage 1

To create a sense of belonging and the beginning of predictable patterns of interaction.

To develop member loyalty to the group.

To create an environment in which members feel safe enough to contribute ideas and suggestions.

The first stage of group development is characterized by members' dependency on the designated leader, concerns about safety, and concerns about feeling included in the group. This first stage of group development may manifest itself as members' compliance with plans proposed by the group leader or by a powerful member. Group members often engage in what has been called pseudowork, or flight, such as exchanging stories about customers or their families that are not relevant to the task at hand. Members also may wait for the group leader to make decisions. In fact, members often urge the leader to take charge and tell them what to do. Members seem more concerned with being accepted by others than with the task at hand. They are unlikely to express different points of view as a result.

Identifying a Stage 1 Group

1. Members are concerned about personal safety in the group.

2. Members are concerned about acceptance and inclusion by others in the group.

3. Members fear rejection.

4. Members communicate in tentative and very polite ways.

5. Members express a need for dependable and directive leadership.

6. Members see the leader as benevolent and competent.

7. Members expect and encourage the leader to provide them with direction and personal safety.

8. The leader is very rarely challenged by the members.

9. The group's goals are not clear to its members, but members don't try to clarify them.

10. Members rarely express disagreement with the group's initial goals.

11. The group assumes that there is consensus about its goals.

12. Role assignments tend to be based on external status, first impressions, and initial self-presentation rather than on matching member competencies with goals and task requirements.

13. Member compliance is high.

14. Communication tends to go through the leader.

15. Participation is generally limited to a few vocal members.

16. Conflict is minimal.

17. Conformity is high.

18. A lack of group structure and organization is evident.

19. Member deviation from emerging norms is rare.

20. Cohesion and commitment to the group are based on identification with the leader.

21. Subgroups and coalitions are rare.

BOX 2.1   Silence of the Lambs

You know you're in a Stage 1 group when the leader asks a question and no one responds. The leader's words seem to vanish into the Bermuda Triangle.

Stage 2: Counterdependency and Fight

Goal of Stage 2

To develop a unified set of goals, values, and operational procedures.

At Stage 2, the group seeks to free itself from its dependence on the leader, and members fight among themselves about group goals and procedures. Task conflict is an inevitable part of this process. The group's task at this stage is to develop a unified set of goals, values, and operational procedures, and this task usually generates conflict. Task conflict is also necessary for the establishment of trust and a climate in which members feel free to disagree with each other.

Some groups become mired in interpersonal conflicts, however, and remain stuck at this developmental stage. Other groups are overwhelmed by the stress of this phase and revert to leader dependence in an attempt to avoid further conflict. Research tells us that task conflict is essential for teams to become effective and productive. Interpersonal conflict, however, can stop a work group in its tracks. When disagreements become personal, trust is lost and members do not feel safe in the group. Stay focused on the work tasks and avoid conflicts based on personality or incompatibility.

Neither remaining stuck in Stage 2 nor regressing to Stage 1 has positive effects for the group or for the quality of work generated by the group. Only through resolution of task conflicts and the development of a unified view of the group's purpose and procedures can true collaboration be achieved.

BOX 2.2   Toxic Waste

You know you're in a Stage 2 group when the thought of going to a team meeting makes you feel ill.

Identifying a Stage 2 Group

1. Conflicts about values emerge.

2. Disagreements about goals and tasks emerge.

3. Increased feelings of safety allow dissent to occur.

4. Dissatisfaction with roles may surface.

5. Clarification of goals begins.

6. Role clarification also begins.

7. Members challenge the leader and each other.

8. Subgroups and coalitions form.

9. Group intolerance of subgroups, cliques, and coalitions is evident.

10. Increased member participation is evident.

11. Decreased conformity begins.

12. Deviation from emerging group norms begins to occur.

13. Attempts at conflict management begin.

14. If efforts to resolve conflicts are successful, increased consensus about group goals and culture becomes evident near the end of this stage.

15. Conflict resolution, if successful, increases trust and cohesion.

Stage 3: Trust and Structure

Goals of Stage 3

To solidify positive relationships among members.

To engage in more mature negotiations about roles and organizational procedures.

If a group manages to work through the inevitable conflicts of Stage 2, member trust, commitment to the group, and willingness to cooperate increase. Communication becomes more open and task oriented. Professional territoriality decreases as members focus more on the task and less on issues of status, power, or influence. This third stage of group development is characterized by more mature negotiations about roles, organization, and procedures. It is also a time in which members work to solidify positive working relationships with each other.

BOX 2.3   How He's Changed!

You know you're in a Stage 3 group when the group member who drove you crazy for weeks begins to make you smile.

Identifying a Stage 3 Group

1. Increased goal clarity and consensus are evident.

2. Roles and tasks are adjusted to increase the likelihood of goal achievement.

3. The leader's role becomes less directive and more consultative.

4. The communication structure becomes more flexible.

5. The content of communication becomes more task oriented.

6. Pressures to conform increase again.

7. Helpful deviation is tolerated.

8. Coalitions and subgroups continue to emerge.

9. Increased tolerance of subgroups, cliques, and coalitions is evident.

10. Cohesion and trust increase.

11. Member satisfaction also increases.

12. Cooperation is more evident.

13. Individual commitment to group goals and tasks is high.

14. Greater division of labor occurs.

15. Conflict continues to occur, but it is managed more effectively.

16. The group works to clarify and build a group structure that will facilitate goal achievement.

Stage 4: Work

Goals of Stage 4

To get the job done well.

To make informed decisions.

To remain cohesive while encouraging task-related conflicts.

To maintain high performance over the long haul.

As its name implies, the fourth stage of group development is a time of intense team productivity and effectiveness. At this stage the group becomes a high performance team. Having resolved many of the issues of the previous stages, the team can focus more of its energy on goal achievement and task accomplishment. Although some work occurs at every developmental stage, the quality and quantity of work increase significantly during Stage 4.

Whenever I teach or give a talk or presentation, I describe Stage 4 and ask the audience members to raise a hand if they have ever been a member of a Stage 4 group. About one in four people raise their hand. This leads me to believe that many readers of this book have never been a member of a Stage 4 group. So, read this next section carefully. Working in a Stage 4 group is a wonderful experience.

Identifying a Stage 4 Group

1. Members are clear about the team's goals.

2. Members agree with the team's goals.

3. Tasks require a team rather than individual effort.

4. Members are clear about their roles.

5. Members accept their roles and status in the team.

6. Role assignments match member abilities.

7. Delegation or "unleadership" is the prevailing leadership style.

8. The team's communication structure matches the demands of the task.

9. The team has an open communication structure in which all members participate and are heard.

10. The team has an appropriate ratio of task and supportive communications.

11. The team gets, gives, and utilizes feedback about its effectiveness and productivity.

12. The team spends time defining problems it must solve or decisions it must make.

13. The team spends time planning how it will solve problems and make decisions.

14. The team spends enough time discussing its problems and decisions.

15. The team determines methods for decision making that are participatory.

16. The team implements and evaluates its decisions and solutions to problems.

17. Voluntary conformity is high.

18. Task-related deviance is tolerated.

19. Team norms encourage high performance and quality.

20. The team expects to be successful.

21. The team encourages innovation.

22. Team members pay attention to the details of their work.

23. The team accepts coalition and subgroup formation.

24. Subgroups are integrated into the team as a whole.

25. Subgroups work on important tasks.

26. Tasks contain variety and challenge.

27. Each subgroup works on a total product or project.

28. The team contains the smallest number of members necessary to accomplish its goals.

29. Subgroups are recognized and rewarded by the team.

30. The team is highly cohesive.

31. Interpersonal attraction among members is high.

32. Members are cooperative.

33. Periods of conflict are frequent but brief.

34. The team has effective conflict management strategies.

BOX 2.4   Pride in the Work

You know you're in a Stage 4 group when you can't wait to get to the team meeting because it's exhilarating, fun, important, and makes you feel like a grown-up.

Group development does not always proceed in a positive direction. Groups can get stuck at a particular stage for an extended period of time, resulting in long-term ineffectiveness and low productivity. Also, groups may fluctuate widely based on the circumstances and forces affecting them at a given moment. Changes in membership, external demands, and changes in leadership can all affect the work of a group. Turnover rates, reassignments, and new upper-level managers often produce regression and require the rebuilding of group structures and culture.

BOX 2.5   The Stages of Group Development

I. Dependency and Inclusion

II. Counterdependency and Fight

III. Trust and Structure

IV. Work and Productivity

Not all work groups, of any type, achieve adequate levels of effectiveness and productivity. In fact, some studies estimate that between 80% and 90% of all groups have difficulties with performance. While achieving an effective performance level is difficult for any group, it is even more problematic for groups with diverse members. Groups composed of members from different professions, for example, have additional obstacles to productivity. These include the lack of an organizing framework, issues of professional territoriality, and miscommunication. The road to productivity is fraught with difficulties.

Surviving Group Development

There are a few things that people can do, and a few attitudes that people can take on, that make the process of group development easier. Like human beings, groups have some rocky times on the road to maturity. Here are a few suggestions to help group members survive, and even enjoy, the process of group development.

- **Learn about group development.**

It helps to know what's in store for you as you move through the various stages of individual human development. For example, once social scientists determined that adults experience developmental stages, some of which are not so pleasant, we all breathed a sigh of relief. Once we started talking about adolescent insecurities, midlife crises, menopause, and the like, many people stopped feeling alone and out of control. Instead of feeling scared or depressed, people felt normal. Other people were experiencing the same things, and that made individuals feel better. Knowledge of developmental stages also makes an individual's experiences at a particular age seem more manageable. Finally, this knowledge usually leads to better, happier individual development.

The same is true of group development. When group members know that all groups go through predictable stages of development, then they can relax and enjoy the ride. When groups don't know about group development, their members might think that their fellow group members are strange or that their particular group is extremely dysfunctional or unusual. Clearly, people with knowledge of group behavior will make better group members and leaders. Such knowledgeable people are less likely to misinterpret what they see and more likely to be constructive in what they say and do.

- **Be patient.**

While human development and group development have a lot in common, group development doesn't take as long. However, it does take some time. My colleagues and I have been monitoring the progress of hundreds of groups over the years, and we have yet to see a high performance team that has been meeting for less than six months. For the first two or three months, groups are dealing with the issues characteristic of Stages 1 and 2. Groups generally enter Stage 3 in the fourth or fifth month, and Stage 4, or high performance, typically begins during the sixth or seventh month. Of course, this assumes that a group doesn't run into any snags.

Most people in upper management and in groups don't understand that groups develop over time. They want groups to be functioning at high levels from the beginning. That simply doesn't happen. It takes time to figure out what the goals really mean. It takes time to figure out how to accomplish those goals and who should do what. It takes time to resolve problems and disagreements that come up. It's important to be patient.

Unfortunately, some groups, like some people, never mature. They stay stuck in dependency or conflict for as long as the group exists. Other groups manage to become high performance teams only to regress to earlier stages later on. This is usually due to some internal crisis or a change in the level of organizational support.

Fortunately, no group has to stay stuck or regressed. If members are willing to work to turn things around, it can be done.

- **Expect things to be murky at the beginning of a group.**

Things are never clear at the beginning of a group. Often, after an early meeting, you'll hear people asking each other questions about what went on during the meeting. Of course, no one asked those questions during the meeting. This is normal, and as time goes on, people will begin to feel free to ask for clarification during group meetings. A person who expects a new group to have a perfectly organized meeting with clear outcomes will be disappointed. This person might even get angry, and that will do no one any good.

- **Expect conflict and treat it as a positive sign of progress.**

Most of us avoid conflict as much as we can. The problem in groups, as in life, is that conflict is inevitable. Each group has to define its goals, clarify how it will function, and determine the various roles that members will play. Group members should expect there to be disagreements about the content of the group's goal and how to solve specific problems related to that goal. Task conflict is a necessary part of this process because, from divergent points of view, one relatively unified direction must be agreed on if group members are to work together in a productive way.

On a more psychological level, task conflict is necessary for the establishment of a safe environment. While, at first glance, this may seem paradoxical, task conflict is helpful to the development of trust. We all know from our own experience that it is easier to develop trust in another person or in a group if we believe that we can disagree and won't be abandoned or hurt because we have a different perspective. It is difficult to trust those who deny us the right to hold different views. To engage in a task conflict with others and to "work it out" is an exhilarating experience. It provides energy, a shared experience, and a sense of safety and authenticity, as well as allowing for deeper trust and collaboration.

From the task perspective, if people are not free to express their points of view, the group's product is likely to be an inferior one. If everyone just goes along with the first idea that's expressed, the outcome is unlikely to be of high quality. Task conflict is a normal, natural, and necessary part of group life. Keeping that in mind will make things much easier.

- **Help the group to limit conflicts to those about tasks, roles, structures, and the like; don't get involved in personal feuds or personality conflicts.**

Although conflict may be normal and necessary, some kinds of conflict can be very detrimental to group development. Personal feuds and personality conflicts that erupt in groups can cause group progress to cease, sometimes permanently. The problem with personal conflicts is that they usually can't be resolved. If one person doesn't like another's personality, the rest of the group can't really do anything about it. However, what appear to be personality conflicts really often result from other factors in the group that can be addressed, such as goal confusion, role assignments, and the like. The group can deal with these things more successfully. In general, it's good to disagree about goals, tasks, roles, and so on. It's not good for group members to personalize these things and see other members as bad or incompetent because they have a different opinion or a different way of doing things.

- **Compromise on issues when possible and help others resolve differences.**

In the course of my research I have attended or listened to tapes of many group meetings. Sometimes members disagree and no one is willing to compromise. While I would not advocate compromise on an issue that is really important to group success or that has ethical consequences, compromise is essential to group productivity.

One example of unwillingness to compromise sticks in my mind. The group was working on a very important new product for the company. The company had had a recent layoff, and more layoffs were anticipated. The group was over budget and had missed several deadlines. During my observation, a conflict unrelated to the goal of the group kept emerging. Members had taken sides on this issue, and neither side was willing to give in. This story has a happy ending. I worked with the group and helped them to see that this conflict about who was right and who was wrong would ultimately result in group failure. Most stories like this don't have happy endings.

- **Don't sit on the sidelines; take responsibility for what's going on, even if it doesn't involve you directly.**

Every group member is responsible for the group's outcomes. Group members shouldn't wait for other members or the leader to solve a problem or save the day. Members should make suggestions and share their ideas, concerns, and hesitations. Of course, it helps if they can do this in a diplomatic way.

- **Be supportive of other members and the leader.**

Research that my colleagues and I have conducted over the years has required us to put each verbal statement made by group members into one of a number of categories. Examples of supportive statements follow:

"Thanks for that suggestion, Joe."

"I appreciate you saying that, Mary."

"I agree with you, Abe."

Out of every 100 statements made by members of groups that are doing well, between 15 and 20 are supportive statements. That sounds like a lot, but we see this over and over. There's nothing like a little support to encourage people to work to capacity.

- **Complete your tasks in a timely fashion.**

Groups are not just groups during meeting times. Group members work together and separately outside of the group to complete work related to the group's goals. Nothing slows down group progress more than when those tasks are not accomplished in a timely fashion. Trust is built among members not by words but by actions. If group members can trust each other to do what they say, things go very smoothly.

- **Don't be upset when subgroups or coalitions emerge.**

Sometimes subgroups are formed because they are necessary to getting a group's work done. At other times, group members form a coalition with others to emphasize a point they're trying to make. This is all natural and good, but the existence of subgroups and coalitions upsets some people. These people may feel left out or believe that the presence of smaller units within the group will interfere with the group's success. Some group members call these subgroups "cliques," which has negative connotations. However, the presence of subgroups is generally not negative. It's a sign that the group is getting organized and will be able to get its work done during the inevitable crunch time. Coalitions can help the group to see another point of view, which often turns out to be the right one.

Of course, subgroups and coalitions can have negative effects sometimes. When coalitions are unwilling to compromise, for example, things can go awry. When subgroups take action without checking with or informing the whole group, the results can be negative. Most of the time, however, the appearance of subgroups and coalitions is a healthy sign of group progress.

- **Encourage your group to regularly assess how it is functioning.**

People at work these days are very busy. They want the meeting to end quickly so that they can deal with the piles of work on their desks. The last thing people want to do is take five minutes out of the meeting to discuss how they're working together. The very last thing they want to do is spend an entire meeting every two months or so discussing how the group is functioning. That seems like a big waste of time. I encourage groups to do it anyway. In the long run, it will save time and aggravation. More on how to assess group progress regularly can be found in Chapter 10.

- **Show up.**

I once worked with a group in which the membership changed almost weekly. There were 20 people in this planning group. Each week about 10 people showed up, and those 10 were different almost every time. There is nothing like an unstable membership to slow group development or to stop it altogether. Each meeting becomes a repeat of the last, where the focus becomes catching people up on what happened at the last meeting.

In later chapters, I will offer more suggestions to members and leaders about what they can do to help their groups be successful. These were just for openers.

THREE

NAVIGATING STAGE 1

⎯⎯•◆•⎯⎯

Goals of Stage 1

Certain behaviors are characteristic of all beginning, or Stage 1, groups. These behaviors can be classified into three categories: concerns about safety and inclusion, member dependency on the designated leader, and a wish for order and structure. Because these categories of behavior happen in all groups during the dependency and inclusion stage, there has to be a reason, or purpose, for their occurrence. If the overall goal of group development is to create an organized unit capable of working effectively to achieve specific ends, then each stage of group development must contribute to that goal in some way. The first step to achieving that overall goal is to create a sense of belonging and the beginnings of predictable patterns of interaction. That is the purpose of Stage 1.

By the end of Stage 1, members should feel a sense of loyalty to the group. They should want to belong to the group, and they should feel safe enough to contribute ideas and suggestions that will, in their opinion, help the group to achieve its overall objectives. If they don't, the group is likely either to disintegrate or to stagnate. Groups disintegrate when members stop attending meetings or participating in group-related activities between meetings. Groups stagnate when the neophyte group system fails to grow and mature.

This chapter describes events that often happen during Stage 1, and what members and leaders can do to make it more likely that group members will emerge from Stage 1 with a sense of belonging and a feeling of safety. Also, through the efforts of members and leaders, the group will have developed rudimentary structures that provide an initial sense of order and predictability.

BOX 3.1   Best Excuse

This group ran the company. The members were the senior vice presidents and the CEO. I was going over the results of a group assessment I had done with them. The group was stuck in Stage 1. While they knew they disagreed about many things, no one was willing to raise controversial issues. In fact, many members didn't talk very much at meetings. I told them things wouldn't change unless they began to discuss these things. The CEO said, "Oh, we forgot to tell you that we took the Myers-Briggs test and all of us scored high on introversion. We're all introverts." I replied, "I don't care if you're aardvarks. You guys run the show. Your cars cost more than people's homes. You have to talk to each other."

Concerns About Safety and Inclusion

The behaviors, feelings, and attitudes that members of new groups express can be summarized as follows:

- Members are concerned about personal safety in the group.
- Members want to be accepted by other members and the leader.
- Members fear rejection.
- Members communicate in tentative and very polite ways.

The following example shows how concerns for safety and inclusion might occur in a new group.

You have been assigned to work in a new group. The first meeting is to be held at 10 o'clock. People begin to arrive a few minutes before 10. You've decided to check things out during this meeting. After all, you know only two people in the room. You smile at a few people and they smile back, but there's not much talking going on. You feel a little awkward, and it's obvious that others do, too. A brave soul asks the person sitting next to him what the purpose of this team is going to be. She shrugs her shoulders. A couple of folks smile and giggle a bit. Someone says, "Adam told me something about it, but I'm not very clear on it. He just said he was putting a group together to work on a new project and he wanted me on the team." Another person says, "That's how it was with me, too." Others nod in agreement and the room falls silent again.

What You Can Do

Now that you know that one of the goals of the first stage of group development is to create a sense of safety and inclusion, there are some things you can do in a situation like this to help the group achieve that goal. You could, for example, introduce yourself to the person next to you and talk about what you do in the organization. If you do this loudly enough, others may introduce themselves as well. If not, ask other people who they are.

When the room falls silent, you could comment on how first meetings are always a little awkward but it usually gets better pretty quickly. Statements like this tend to make others feel more comfortable and stimulate further conversation. The key is to keep the goal in mind (safety and inclusion) and act in ways that increase the likelihood of achieving that goal. Don't wait for others to act. Don't wait for the leader to act. Remember that everyone is responsible for the achievement of group goals. So, just do it.

Dependency on the Designated Leader

- Members express a need for dependable and directive leadership.
- The leader is seen as benevolent and competent.
- The leader is expected and encouraged to provide members with direction and personal safety.
- The leader is very rarely challenged.
- Cohesion and commitment to the group are based on identification with the leader.

The following example shows how these issues might occur in a new group.

After a few minutes, Adam arrives. He stops to greet a few people as he walks into the room. Everyone seems grateful for his arrival. You think to yourself that Adam is the designated leader of this new group and he will get the ball rolling. Just his arrival seems to have made a difference. People seem more relaxed already. They are all looking at Adam, smiling, and waiting for him to speak.

Adam doesn't waste any time. He doesn't even ask people to introduce themselves. Since he knows everyone, he assumes others know each other as well. Instead, he begins to outline the tasks of the group and the time line in which tasks have to be accomplished. Some people begin to look a little confused, and others seem a bit tense. No one says anything, though.

What You Can Do

At this stage, dependence on the leader is normal. Members expect Adam to take charge. You don't want to undermine Adam's authority or credibility at this point, but you do want to help him do a good job. Adam has forgotten to do a few things. In the best of all possible worlds, Adam would have introduced himself and asked others to do the same. He would have stated the agenda of the meeting and handed out copies of that agenda. He would have stated the goal of the group and launched a discussion about that goal.

If you are the leader of a new group, don't make Adam's mistakes. Come to the meeting prepared. Make sure people are introduced in enough depth that they learn not just one another's names but also what each person does and what each does well. Provide a detailed agenda that includes a written statement of the group's goal. Spend the first meeting discussing that goal.

Since Adam forgot to do those things, you could help him and the group by asking for introductions. It helps to say something like, "Adam, I may be the only one, but I don't know everybody. Can we introduce ourselves before we get started?"

In a similar fashion, you might ask to know the agenda of the meeting and request clarification of the group's goal. Usually you won't have to ask all these questions. Others will chime in once the ice is broken. The key is to keep this goal in mind as well. At this point, the group needs a dependable, directive, and competent leader. Help Adam to meet that group need.

If you are the leader and members ask questions, make suggestions, or point out things you have forgotten to do, thank them for their help. Don't get defensive or embarrassed, even if a member says something in a way that seems rude or challenging. Assume group members are trying to be helpful and encourage them to participate. In the long run, you'll be happy you did.

Some groups don't have designated leaders. This problem can slow group progress. If this is the case in your group, suggest that a group coordinator be chosen. Research suggests that leaderless groups have more difficulty getting organized and more difficulty progressing through the stages of group development.

Desire for Order and Structure

- Goals are not clear to members, but clarification is not sought.
- Members rarely express disagreement with initial group goals.
- Group members assume consensus about goals exists.
- Role assignments tend to be based on external status, first impressions, and initial self-presentation rather than on matching member competencies with goal and task requirements.
- Member compliance is high.
- Communication tends to go through the leader.
- Participation is generally limited to a few vocal members.
- Conflict is minimal.
- Conformity is high.
- A lack of group structure and organization is evident.
- Member deviation from emerging norms is rare.
- Subgroups and coalitions are rare.

The following example shows how these issues might occur in a new group.

Adam responds to your request and states the goal of the group. He asks if people are clear about the goal, and everyone nods. You remain a little confused about the goal but, because everyone seems to understand what's expected, you don't say anything. Adam returns to outlining the tasks of the group and the time line in which tasks have to be accomplished. He asks for volunteers to take on the various tasks.

What You Can Do

From reading this book, you know that if goals are not perfectly clear and accepted by everybody, the chances of group success are limited. You also know that planning how to accomplish tasks and discussing who should do each task are crucial to group success.

Finally, you know that making sure input is sought from all group members increases the chances of group success. So, you ask Adam and the group members to discuss their understanding of the goal in a little more depth. Later you raise the issue of role assignments. It's best to raise this issue by inquiring about your own role, especially if it doesn't seem appropriate to you based on your skills and abilities. Of course, chances are slim that you will have to raise all these issues. By now, other members will be raising issues as well.

A word of advice for leaders is in order here. You know that discussing goals at length, spending time planning how to accomplish tasks, and assigning tasks based on member skills are important to group success. Make sure these things happen, but don't hog the limelight. Remember that it's good to see members raise issues and not have to raise all those issues yourself. Don't be too perfect, and don't be too dominant. Provide for member safety. Provide initial direction and support members' attempts to participate.

This chapter has provided examples of events that typically occur in Stage 1 groups. It hasn't been meant to cover all possible scenarios. The real intention of this chapter and those that follow is to help members and leaders develop a framework to guide their actions in groups. The framework is pretty simple. Know the goals of each stage of development and act in ways that will help your group achieve those goals. If the members and leaders described in this chapter follow that advice, the group will move forward. People will develop a sense of belonging and safety, members will begin to trust Adam's leadership skills, and the beginnings of order will appear. The group will be ready to move on.

⊰ FOUR ⊱

SURVIVING STAGE 2

⸻⸱⬩⸱⸻

Goals of Stage 2

Having safely navigated the first stage of group development, members and the leader have developed an initial sense of loyalty to the group. Some degree of organization has begun to emerge, and people feel safer speaking up in the group. Now some hard work has to be done. If the group is to become a unit capable of performing at high levels, then members and the leader both need to create a unified group culture and an effective organizational structure in which to work.

Group culture refers to a set of shared perceptions or assumptions about values, norms, and goals. These assumptions, once established, dictate how people will behave and the kind of organizational structure the group will require to express its cultural assumptions and achieve its goals.

In the first stage of group development, members were primarily concerned about personal safety and feeling included. Preliminary discussions probably focused on how people should interact in the group and how members should organize themselves to accomplish tasks. More discussion will be needed, however, to reach agreement about these things. Every member will have to participate for this to occur.

The second stage of group development is described as a period of counterdependency and fight. This is so because conflict with the leader and among group members is inevitable if the goals of Stage 2 are to be reached. The group's goal at this stage is to develop a unified set of goals, values, and operational procedures, and this goal usually generates conflict. Differences of opinion are very likely to occur. Conflict is also necessary in order to establish a trusting climate in which members feel free to disagree with each other.

Some groups become mired in conflict and remain stuck at this developmental stage. Other groups are overwhelmed by the stress of this phase and revert to leader dependence in an attempt to avoid further conflict. Neither of these outcomes has positive effects for the group or for the quality of work that will be generated by the group. Only through conflict resolution and the development of a unified view of the group's purpose and processes can true collaboration be achieved.

This chapter briefly describes events that often happen during Stage 2 and what members and leaders can do to increase the likelihood that group members will emerge from this stage with a shared culture and an organizational structure that will enable them to be productive and successful. It also describes how working to achieve the goals of Stage 2 increases trust among group members and makes working together more enjoyable as well as more effective.

A Unified Group Culture

The first thing a group needs to do during Stage 2 is to begin to create a unified group culture. Here are some things that will happen as a group attempts to do this:

- Conflicts about values emerge.
- Disagreements about goals and tasks emerge.
- Increased feelings of safety allow dissent to occur.
- Members challenge the leader and each other.
- Clarification of goals begins.
- Decreased conformity begins.
- Deviation from emerging group norms begins.

The following examples show how these issues might occur in a Stage 2 group.

The group has been meeting for about eight weeks. Nina, the group's leader, is going over a list of things the group needs to work on in the coming weeks if they're to stay on schedule. Suddenly, Jack says, "I'm not sure about this, Nina. How can they expect us to come up with such a complicated policy in such a short time? I'm not even sure a policy will solve this problem. I'm not convinced this is the right way to go." A few other members nod their heads in agreement with Jack.

Nina is stunned. She thought all members had agreed to the group's goal weeks ago. She wonders if this is just a power play on Jack's part or if he really means it.

What You Can Do

This kind of situation occurs quite often in Stage 2 groups. When people say the group seems to be going in circles or rehashing topics that have already been discussed and resolved, it's usually because of situations like this. People are in a hurry to get on with things. They easily get upset with members who revisit issues they think have been decided already.

Instead of getting frustrated or angry with an individual or two, try to remember two things. First, remember that when things were initially discussed, the group was in Stage 1. Some people didn't feel safe enough to express disagreement at that point. It seemed like everyone agreed, but not everyone expressed her or his opinion. Later on, when feelings of safety have increased, disagreements get voiced. This is a good thing.

Second, when a group is faced with a complicated set of goals and tasks, it takes people time to examine those goals and tasks thoroughly. Forming opinions doesn't happen quickly, especially if those opinions are important to individual and group success. It's a good thing to revisit issues after members have had time to think. It's a very good thing, actually. Many decisions and agreements made in haste have been the wrong ones.

Whether you're a member or the leader of this group, it would help if you said something like, "I'm glad Jack brought this up. It makes a lot of sense to discuss our goals and objectives again to make sure everybody's on the same page." This may be hard for Nina to say, since she may think Jack's comments were meant as an attack on her leadership. It would be wise of her to say it anyway. If Nina doesn't say it, a member should try to ward off a potentially negative argument between these two people. The issue isn't whether Jack is trying to undermine Nina's authority. He may or may not be doing that. It doesn't matter. What matters for the group at this stage in its development is to make sure that everyone agrees with, and understands, the group's goal.

The group had developed the habit of holding lunch meetings. Jane didn't like this, since she usually worked out at the company's gym during lunch. She skipped a meeting and went to the gym. Other members were appalled and confronted her about her lack of commitment to the group at the next meeting. Jane said that she didn't like the meeting time because it infringed on her personal time. She even said she bet other people were unhappy with the meeting time, too. A couple of people agreed with Jane. Some just shook their heads.

What You Can Do

During Stage 1, many norms get established without much discussion. In this case, it's likely that meeting during lunch worked well for the group leader. In Stage 1, people tend to go along with whatever the leader proposes. So, lunchtime meetings became the norm. As the group developed and people began to feel more comfortable with each other, those who didn't like the meeting time became more vocal. This, too, is a good thing.

If group norms undermine people's motivation to attend or participate in the group, changes are in order. Finding a mutually agreeable meeting time in a busy workplace is challenging. It's important, though. If members skip meetings, the effects on the group will be negative. A large part of each meeting will be devoted to catching people up on what occurred at the last meeting. This will slow down or stop group progress. If people attend but are resentful of the meeting time, they will not participate fully and may act in unproductive ways.

If a situation like this occurs in your group, it would be helpful to say something like, "I think we should try to find a meeting time that fits everyone's schedule. How's Tuesday at three?"

Many norms that emerge during the first stage of group development will be challenged in the second stage. The next example demonstrates how this may happen.

Lora tends to go on and on at meetings. Whatever the topic, she has an opinion, which she expresses in great detail. You want to express an opinion as well, and you know that other people would like to air their views. No one interrupts Lora, however. Everyone just sits and fidgets or stares straight ahead. No one feels able to give feedback to anyone else about his or her behavior in the group. Although it's never been voiced, everyone knows that giving feedback violates some unstated rule. Members feel they have to be nice and tolerant in this group.

What You Can Do

Generally speaking, being nice and tolerant of others is a good norm to establish. If it means that the group will fail to achieve its work goals, however, then the norm is too strict and should be altered. As people begin to feel safer, they will start to voice disagreement with norms and suggest elimination or alteration of some norms. In fact, this must occur if the group is to develop a culture that will support group goal achievement.

In this case, you could say something like the following: "Lora, I think I understand your position on this and I want to hear from others as well before I make up my mind. What do the rest of you think about this?" You'll probably feel a little uncomfortable doing this because you're breaking a group rule. Keep in mind, though, that if Lora is allowed to monopolize the conversation for much longer, the frustrations of others will continue to mount. Eventually, someone (maybe even you) will explode and confront Lora in a very negative way. The confrontation may get very personal and precipitate a feud in the group. Some members will rush to Lora's defense, and others may join the attack against her. This not only will be a colossal waste of group time but also will be very hurtful to Lora and group morale. It's better to intervene early in a situation like this. Do so with all the diplomacy you can muster. Be gentle. Don't blame Lora for her behavior. Focus on what the group needs to do to accomplish its goals.

These examples emphasize two important things about norms. First, don't make norms about unimportant things. Adopting too many norms is like having too many laws in a society. If every aspect of group life is legislated, people feel constrained. They won't feel free to express themselves, which seriously limits input and creativity. Ultimately, this will decrease the chances of group success.

Second, scrutinize norms for their contribution to group effectiveness and productivity. If they don't measure up, eliminate or modify them. Norms are necessary to create predictable patterns of behavior and similarity in member values and attitudes. They must relate to goals and objectives, however. If norms interfere with achievement and high performance, change them.

Gordon, the leader of the group, has just laid out his plan to increase sales in a specific region. Walter, the sales director in that region, reacts by saying, "You just don't get it, Gordon. What you're proposing won't work in a million years! If you had any sense of the history of this problem or the people in my region, you'd know that. When was the last time you met with us? Was it two or three years ago?"

What You Can Do

This is one of the scarier moments in group life. A member has attacked the leader in a very personal and confrontational way. This kind of confrontation doesn't always happen. In groups that are ultimately successful, disagreements with the leader happen quite a lot, but they are generally milder, more tactful, and do not challenge the leader's competence or intelligence.

Challenging the leader is an essential part of group life. If group members always accept the leader's views, there is no reason to have a group at all. A major reason for working in groups is the assumption that decisions made by groups will be better than those made by the best and brightest group member alone. That is, collective intelligence is assumed to be greater than individual intelligence. While I am not sure this is always the case, it is the case in a high performance team. For a group to utilize collective intelligence and become a high performance team, the dominance of the leader must be reduced so that others can contribute to that collective intelligence. Disagreements with leaders are necessary at times to produce the best decisions and to achieve at high levels.

Obviously, the manner in which a member disagrees with a leader—or another member, for that matter—is key. In the current example, Walter not only disagrees with Gordon's plan, but he also challenges Gordon personally. He chastises Gordon for his lack of knowledge about the region and for his lack of attention to regional problems. This type of conflict can be very destructive to a group. Some members will be frightened by this situation. Feelings of safety, so essential to group unity, will be undermined, and some members may retreat into silence. Other members may jump to Gordon's defense. Still others may side with Walter in opposition to Gordon. This could lead to an irreparable split in the group. It could spell doom for the group if the split cannot be repaired.

You must act quickly to keep these things from happening. Keep a few things in mind as you do this. First, in all likelihood, Gordon is hurt and angry because of what Walter has said. He may also be embarrassed by this public challenge to his leadership and will want to save face. Walter probably is feeling angry, a little embarrassed about his outburst, and anxious about what Gordon will do in response. You should proceed with caution in this emotional situation. You should act, however, because this situation could have very negative effects on the group.

Say something like the following: "I know what it's like to feel loyal to the people back home, Walter. It's hard for any of us to know what really is going on there. All of us, including Gordon, want you to lay out your plans to increase sales. Maybe some others have ideas to contribute, too. Is that okay with everybody?"

Your intention in making a statement like this is to refocus the group on developing a plan to increase sales and to defuse the tension between Gordon and Walter. If your intervention works, the focus will return to the task at hand. You will probably get a lot of help from other group members once you say this. Other members will be eager to reduce the mounting tension.

Earlier in this book, I talked about how important it is to avoid getting involved in personality conflicts and personal fights. This example makes clear why this is so important. Nothing threatens group success more than destructive personal arguments.

If you find yourself in a position similar to Walter's, don't do what he did. This situation could have been avoided if Walter had said the following: "I see what your plan is based on, Gordon, but I want to update you on some current issues in the region. Some things have happened that you may not be aware of."

If you find yourself in Gordon's situation someday, and someone like Walter challenges you in a negative way, remember that a leader's job is to work for the good of the group. It would be in the group's best interest for you to say, "You're right, Walter, I may not be aware of some recent developments. Tell me what's been going on lately." This is not easy to do when you are feeling unduly attacked. It's not easy to stifle your urge to retaliate. No one said leadership was easy, however. Do what's best for the group.

A Unified and Effective Group Structure

As Stage 2 groups begin to create an effective group structure, the following things are likely to occur:

- Dissatisfaction with roles surfaces.
- Role clarification begins.
- Disagreements about strategies to accomplish group tasks surface.
- Disagreements about how to make decisions emerge.
- Subgroups and coalitions form.
- Group intolerance of subgroups, cliques, and coalitions is evident.
- Increased member participation is evident.
- Attempts at conflict management begin.

- Increased consensus about goals and culture becomes evident near the end of this stage.
- Conflict resolution, if successful, increases trust and cohesion.

The following examples show how these issues might occur in a Stage 2 group.

In one of the early meetings, Penny, the group leader, asked you to investigate the budget implications of increasing the sales force in a certain area. At the time, you agreed to do it. After a while, you began to feel uncomfortable with the assignment because you're unfamiliar with the product line in that area. You believe Jean would do a better job but don't know how to bring this up.

What You Can Do

Perhaps the best way to handle this situation is to approach Penny outside the meeting and say something like this: "I'm feeling a little queasy about my assignment. Jean is more familiar with the product line in that area than I am. She might do a better job. I think she's working on getting the figures for the ad campaign. I'm pretty up on that. Maybe we could switch? If you think it's a good idea, we could suggest a switch at the next meeting."

If the role you are in doesn't match your abilities and talents, try to negotiate for one that does. In the long run, the group will benefit from having the right people in the right roles. Don't avoid challenges, though. Another way to deal with this might be to team up with Jean to work on your assignment. You might learn a lot that way. Whether you switch with or team up with Jean should depend on the group's needs. If time is of the essence, switching is probably best. If developing group members with multiple skills is important to group success, working with Jean on the assignment might be best.

The group is discussing what to do about a particularly difficult decision it must make. Mary breaks into the conversation and says, "I thought we decided this last week. Doesn't anybody else remember that? This happens all the time. We keep revisiting our decisions. They never seem to stick. No wonder we're behind schedule."

What You Can Do

This situation is common in groups. Typically, the reason for this is that the group has developed a very informal decision-making process. Sometimes, it's so informal that some members don't even know when a decision is being made. There was a time when minutes were taken at every group meeting. There also was a time when votes were taken and members raised their hands to signify their position. Over the years, such practices have been abandoned in favor of more informal meeting procedures. The results of this informality are not always positive. Groups need clear decision-making processes that members accept. How groups make decisions may vary. There is no best decision-making process that should be used in all cases. Regardless of which decision-making process is chosen, however, members and the leader should agree to that process in advance.

In this case, an informal process has been enacted and I would bet this was done with no discussion. Like many other aspects of group structure, it just happened without much thought or discussion. You could help in this situation by saying something like, "I remember, Mary, but some people don't. That worries me. Maybe we should make a list of recent decisions we've made to see what we all remember. It also might be a good idea to talk about how we want to make decisions and whether we should record the decisions that we make."

In an effort to get tasks done faster, group members have decided to delegate some tasks to a subgroup of three members. These three are to report back to the group when they have finished. Lately, however, some members have become a little irritated with, and suspicious of, members of the subgroup. They wonder what they're doing and seem to feel excluded by them. They even seem to resent the fact that "The Group of Three" tends to talk with each other more than with the rest of the members.

What You Can Do

Establishing subgroups is a logical way to increase group output and task performance. Division of labor is necessary whenever complex tasks need to be completed in a timely manner. Logical though it may be, it is usually perceived by others as a threat to group unity and cohesion. This is a normal human response. Remember how it felt in high school when you were not invited to join a popular clique? Even if you didn't really want to be part of that group, it didn't feel good to be excluded. We may be all grown up, but some of those feelings remain. Most people want to be in on things. We want to know what others are doing. We want to belong.

In a Stage 2 group, trust is just beginning to build. Members have not developed enough faith in the trustworthiness of their colleagues to be certain that a subset of them would work for the good of the whole group. Maybe they are looking out for themselves or talking about other members in their private meetings! While this may sound paranoid, human beings do have a bit of a paranoid streak.

There are two options in situations like this. The group could choose not to employ subgroups to accomplish tasks, or members could use the emergence of subgroups as an opportunity to increase group trust and cohesion. Obviously, I endorse the latter. The emergence of subgroups is very important to group effectiveness. It's a sign that the group is getting organized, and an organized group is much more likely to be successful. Learning to tolerate and to trust subgroups, then, is vital to group success.

If you are not a member of the subgroup and you have noticed that other nonmembers (perhaps yourself included) are uncomfortable with subgroup members, you might say something like the following: "We're not very comfortable yet with delegating tasks to subgroups. Maybe it would help if the subgroups we created reported more frequently about what they're working on. That might help them stay on track and help the rest of us feel more comfortable. It also would give subgroup members the opportunity to get some input from us and give us some ideas as well."

If you are a member of the subgroup and you have noticed that others seem a little uncomfortable with you, you could raise the same issue by saying, "The three of us have been thinking we'd like to keep you up to date about what we're doing. Could we get five minutes on the agenda to fill you in and ask for advice if we need it?"

Also, if you are a member of a subgroup, keep your commitments. If you are to report back to the whole group on a given date, do so. This is always important, but especially important for the first few subgroups. If early subgroups keep other members and leaders informed of their progress and keep their commitments, group trust and cohesion will increase significantly.

Marie and Tim are arguing about the best way to raise money for the new wing of the museum. Grants and state funding will provide 60% of what's needed. The museum staff must raise the rest. Each believes that her or his way will raise the most money in the shortest time. The rest of the staff have taken sides, and the disagreement is pretty intense.

What You Can Do

Conflict resolution is an essential component of group success. If this becomes a long, drawn-out disagreement, nobody benefits. You can help in this situation by saying something like this: "Let's stop for a minute and outline both plans in detail. Then we can see what we're really talking about in terms of investment of money and staff time. Who knows? Maybe there's a way to combine aspects of both plans. We won't know that, though, until we go over each plan in detail. What do the rest of you think?"

The second stage of group development can be difficult. The goals of this stage are not easy. On U.S. coins is the phrase *e pluribus unum*, which means "from many, one." From many individuals with many points of view, one group must be forged with a coherent culture and structure that will facilitate goal achievement. This is no easy task, but it is made less difficult if members know what to expect and how to help each other accomplish it.

BOX 4.1   Holy War

An interfaith group of priests, nuns, and ministers were in conflict. The male priests and ministers blamed the nuns for the group's problem. They accused the nuns of being too enamored of discussion and dialogue. The men felt that all this talk was going nowhere. After I worked with this group for a while, it became clear that the real problem was that the group didn't have a clear decision-making procedure. Once a decision-making procedure was in place, peace was restored.

FIVE

REORGANIZING AT STAGE 3

‒•◆•‒

Goals of Stage 3

If a group manages to work through the inevitable conflicts of Stage 2, then members' trust, commitment to the group, and willingness to cooperate increase. Communication becomes more open and task oriented. Members focus more on the task and less on issues of status, power, or influence. This third stage of group development, referred to as the trust and structure phase, is characterized by more mature negotiations about roles, organization, and procedures. It is also a time in which members work to solidify positive relationships with each other.

Some things that happen during Stage 3 are described next.

Fine-Tuning Roles, Organization, and Procedures

In the process of fine-tuning roles, the level of organization, and group procedures, the following things are likely to occur:

- Increased goal clarity and consensus about goals are evident.
- Roles and tasks are adjusted to increase the likelihood of goal achievement.
- The leader's role becomes less directive and more consultative.
- The communication structure becomes more flexible.
- The content of communication becomes more task oriented.
- Increased tolerance of subgroups, cliques, and coalitions is evident.

- Greater division of labor occurs.
- Conflict continues to occur, but it is managed more effectively.

The following examples show how these issues might occur in a Stage 3 group.

Phyllis, the group's leader, is actively engaged in the group's discussion. A member named John is running the meeting. Phyllis brings up some new ideas but, after some discussion, the group decides to go with another plan. Then the group runs into a snag. Members are unsure how to implement the plan. Everyone turns to Phyllis for her input.

What You Can Do

At the third stage of group development, leaders are not as prominent as they were in earlier stages. By this time, members are beginning to take over some leadership functions. In this example, a member is running the meeting, which allows the leader to participate more actively in the discussion. Members are much more comfortable with and generally less dependent on the leader for direction. This way of operating is new for the group, however, and there will be moments when the group may revert to previous ways of behaving. In this case, when the group could not reach a decision, members looked to the leader for direction.

This situation is very normal and quite common. Development does not proceed in one direction. We often take two steps forward and one step back. The members and the leader should be mindful of this tendency but not overly concerned. On the other hand, members and leaders should strive to support forward motion. If Phyllis makes this decision for the group, it will not be the end of the world, but it may slow progress a little.

If you are a member of the group, you could help by saying something like, "Hey, let's try to resolve this issue as a group. There's no need to put this on Phyllis. We've dealt with tougher issues than this before." Obviously, you should make this statement with good humor and a smile.

If you are Phyllis, you may feel the urge to "save the group" by making the decision. Try to resist that urge. It would probably be best to say something like, "Let's discuss this a while longer and see what we come up with."

Todd just came back from a fishing trip. He's telling "fish stories" that are pretty funny. Everyone is enjoying listening to him. He's been talking for about five minutes and the meeting is scheduled to last an hour. A number of issues must be dealt with in that hour.

What You Can Do

Having a bit of fun at a meeting is a positive thing and a sign that people are comfortable with each other. It reduces stress and can increase feelings of cohesion. When the fun goes on too long, however, productivity may be compromised. In a Stage 3 group, members are very interested in work. Their conversations are more task oriented and everyone is interested in being efficient and productive. The group is not a high performance team yet, but members want the group to reach high levels of productivity.

There is nothing inherently wrong with Todd's fish stories. However, if you are beginning to worry about getting work done, or if you sense that others are, you might say, "Todd, these stories are wonderful, but it's time for us to get to work."

Annette has just returned from a meeting with Nancy, the vice president, and other project leaders. She reports the details of the meeting to the group members. She's a little worried because two coordinating groups are being set up to oversee aspects of the overall contract. Annette feels stretched to the max and says, "I don't know how I can attend all these meetings, get my other work done, and be responsible to the group."

What You Can Do

One of the hallmarks of a Stage 3 group is that members begin to take on aspects of the leadership role. One important aspect of that role is to communicate and negotiate with other parts of the organization. Groups can lose their way if members don't maintain open communications with other groups that are relevant to their success.

In today's workplace, everyone is busy. Most people I run into feel overloaded. Interacting with other relevant groups, however, is important to group success. You could help by saying something like, "Annette, maybe a few of us could represent our group at those meetings. Someone needs to go, but I don't think it has to be you."

Solidifying Positive Relationships

In the process of building positive relationships among group members, the following things are likely to occur:

- Cohesion and trust increase.
- Member satisfaction increases.
- Cooperation is more evident.
- Individual commitment to group goals and tasks is high.
- Voluntary conformity with group norms increases.
- Helpful deviation is tolerated.

The following examples show how these things might occur in a Stage 3 group.

Al is an odd duck. He doesn't say much during meetings and seems to spend his time doodling on a notepad. For the first few months, group members were uncomfortable with Al and rarely asked for his opinion. After all, he didn't seem to care enough to participate. Every once in a while, though, Al would say something that was right on and very helpful. When it comes to engine design, he really knows his stuff.

What You Can Do

This group has developed a strong norm for participation, and that is a very good thing. It's difficult to develop a high performance team without the participation of the majority of members. For whatever reason, Al is not a talker. This makes others uncomfortable with him, and they question his commitment to the group. They don't perceive him as a team player. On the other hand, when Al does say something, it's worth listening to and usually very helpful.

Ignoring Al or insisting that he become a more active participant will not help the situation. Al is Al, after all. You could help by noticing the kinds of input Al contributes and asking him for his thoughts when those topics come up. You could say, "Al knows more about this than any of us. Can you help us out with this, Al?"

People are different. Some of us are talkers and some of us are not. Some of us follow rules and norms to the letter. Some of us don't. As long as people are making a positive contribution to the group, however small, let them be. The workplace values conformity, and some degree of conformity is necessary if groups are to be successful, but too much conformity can be a negative. If we are all behaving and thinking the same way, generating new ideas may be difficult. Sometimes, oddball ideas are the best ideas.

BOX 5.1   Strangest Goal

I asked a team what their goal was, and they said, in unison, "To be a cohesive team." I asked them if the company paid them well for their efforts.

Some people in the group are expressing concern about whether Colleen, Barbara, and Chris will finish their report on time. They didn't come to the meeting today and no one knows why.

What You Can Do

By the third stage of group development, trust is pretty high. There will be moments, however, when feelings of mistrust surface. This is natural, especially when time is of the essence. You know people like Colleen, Barbara, and Chris. They're just worried about staying on schedule.

You could help by saying something like, "Colleen, Barbara, and Chris will get it done. They're as worried about deadlines as we are. They may need some help, though. I'd be willing to check in with them this week and offer a hand if they need it."

Brigid was asked by the group to fill in the details of a new insurance product members are considering. She's been working on it for two weeks. At the meeting, Brigid says, "I've got most of the details worked out, but a few things have me stumped. I could use some help."

What You Can Do

In the competitive world of business, asking for help is not easy. Brigid's request for help is a sign that she trusts other group members and that she is committed to doing the best possible job. This is terrific and should be encouraged.

You could help by saying something like, "Can you tell us what has you stumped? I'm sure one of us could help. If not, someone probably knows who to go to for the answers."

The third stage of group development is a time when group processes and procedures are adjusted so that the group can work at higher levels of performance. Some issues were already resolved at Stage 2, but other norms, strategies, and roles need to be scrutinized to ensure that they contribute to group achievement.

Now that group members have resolved many earlier issues, trust has increased. Members feel comfortable enough to question how the group is functioning and to suggest changes to increase the chances of success. It's a time to get more organized and to plan better ways of working together. It's also the time to solidify working relationships among members.

One word of caution is necessary here. Some groups enter Stage 3 and focus too much energy on building relationships and not enough on getting organized. These groups begin to resemble love-ins after a while. Members are so busy supporting each other that they forget to make sure the way they're working together is the best way. Research suggests that members should spend about 15% to 20% of group time supporting each other, and the rest should be focused as much as possible on work. Other groups focus too much energy on getting organized and forget to support and encourage each other in that endeavor. That's a classic formula for burnout. If members don't feel supported by the group and others external to the group, they will become disillusioned and resentful. If that happens, the group will find itself back at Stage 2 in a flash.

⊰ SIX ⊱

SUSTAINING HIGH PERFORMANCE

---◦•◉•◦---

Goals of Stage 4

As its name implies, the fourth, or work, stage of group development is a time of intense productivity and effectiveness. At this stage, a work group becomes a team. Having resolved most of the issues of the previous stages, the team can focus most of its energy on goal achievement and task accomplishment. Although work occurs at every developmental stage, the quality and quantity of work increase significantly during Stage 4.

The goals of Stage 4 include getting the work done well, making decisions, remaining cohesive while encouraging task-related conflicts, and maintaining high performance over the long haul.

Sadly, many people have never been a member of a Stage 4 team. They don't know what it's like to work at high performance levels and to enjoy the experience. Some teams that make it to Stage 4 contain members for whom this is a new experience. These members are excited by the ease with which work gets done. They are thrilled with the feelings of camaraderie and trust generated by the team. They are happy they are learning so much and eager for this experience to continue for as long as possible. The problem is that unless members are careful, backsliding may occur.

BOX 6.1   Pride Cometh...

Two groups were working on similar projects. They asked for feedback on how they were doing. I assessed both groups and gave them suggestions on how to improve. The Stage 3 group used the feedback and worked hard to improve. The Stage 4 team didn't. They felt they were doing great and would beat the other group easily. They did not.

44

Getting to Stage 4 is not easy. Many groups never do. Staying at Stage 4 isn't easy, either. Without constant vigilance, teams may regress to earlier stages of development. To maintain high levels of performance for an extended period, team members need to learn some things and to do some things that will keep their effectiveness and performance at high levels. Some of the things high performance teams do to remain effective are described next.

Getting the Work Done Well

The norms in high performance teams support not only getting the work done but also getting the work done well. Those norms include the following:

- Team norms encourage high performance and quality.
- The team expects to be successful.
- The team encourages innovation.
- The team pays attention to the details of its work.

The following examples show how these norms are enacted in high performance teams.

Felice has just suggested a way to get things done faster by eliminating a few steps where quality checks are made. After all, there are other points in the process where the quality is checked. She believes this will save valuable time and some money as well. You are not sure this is a good idea.

What You Can Do

One of the goals of a Stage 4 team is to get the work done well. Norms for quality and high performance have been established and everyone wants to do the best job possible. You know that Felice does as well. She also wants to save time and money, which is not a bad idea if it can be done without compromising quality. Felice's idea will save money. There's no doubt of that. You're not so sure how her plan will affect product quality, however.

Given that the goal is to get the work done well, you might say something like, "Felice, I think we should go over your plan very carefully. I'm as eager as you are to save money and time. I just want to make sure that product quality won't be affected."

The point of saying this is to remind everyone of the norm for quality as well as for high performance. As work intensifies and deadlines loom, it's easy to forget commitments to quality. Gentle reminders are very helpful.

Felice agrees with you that quality is important and describes her plan in more detail. She says there are enough checks at other points in the process to ensure that quality is not compromised. You and other team members are impressed with Felice's careful evaluation of the steps in the process. She really did her homework.

What You Can Do

Part of getting the job done well is to encourage team members to be innovative. Felice has come up with an innovative idea, and, after lengthy team discussion, members think the idea is a good one. You might say, "Felice, I didn't understand at first but you've made a believer out of me. I say we go with your idea. What do the rest of you think?"

Renaya is feeling overwhelmed by the team's current workload. She says, "I'm not sure we can do all this by the end of the month. It seems like too much for us to handle."

What You Can Do

Even members of Stage 4 teams can become anxious about team success. Teams also can set goals for themselves that are too ambitious. The feeling that the team will succeed is vital to high performance. If teams become uncertain about goal achievement, there will be negative repercussions. You want the team to maintain its expectation of success. You also want to address Renaya's concern. You might say, "Renaya, I think we should review our plans for the month. Maybe they are too ambitious. Maybe we haven't divided the workload evenly enough. It could be that you got more than your share. What do the rest of you think about this?"

The team is planning a meeting with the production team to establish the time frame for launching a new product. Dan has been given the responsibility for working out the agenda with George, who heads the production team. Dan has just presented the agenda to the group. Jane says, "Dan I think the agenda includes most of what we need to clear up, but I'm a little concerned about coordinating marketing and production time lines. Shouldn't marketing be included in that meeting?"

What You Can Do

Because paying attention to details is an important component of group success, you might say something like this: "I agree with Jane, Dan. Marketing should be represented at the meeting. I also think it would be a good idea to go over the agenda again to make doubly sure we've covered everything and have all the right players at the meeting." If you are Dan, don't get defensive. People are not trying to find fault with your work. In Stage 4 teams, everyone is committed to getting the work done well. Reviewing plans and checking things twice are an expression of that commitment.

Making Decisions

Decision making in high performance teams is a careful process that involves the following:

- The team spends time defining problems it must solve or decisions it must make.
- The team spends time planning how it will solve problems and make decisions.
- The team spends enough time discussing problems that must be solved and decisions that must be made.
- The team determines methods for decision making that are participatory.
- The team implements and evaluates its solutions and decisions.

Examples of how high performance teams make decisions and what you can do to help are provided next.

Kate says, "Can't we just change the schedule of the show so that it doesn't occur on the same weekend as the Motherwell exhibit at the museum? I don't want our artist to be overshadowed by anything." Mike says, "I agree with you, but I'm worried about what that will do to the whole schedule."

What You Can Do

The team is about to make a decision. You know that in order to make a good decision, the team needs to define the problem clearly. It may seem that the problem is clear. Another institution has scheduled an exhibit that may keep people from attending your institution's art exhibit. Before rearranging your schedule, however, it would make sense to make sure you have defined the problem correctly. You might say, "You could be right that the Motherwell show will compete with ours. I'd feel better, though, if we talked about that a little before we start thinking of solutions."

Lise has a different take on the situation. She thinks that the Motherwell show will attract different people. Midge disagrees. She says, "Motherwell has earned a place in art history. Even people who are not particularly attracted to his work will go to the exhibit because of his stature in contemporary art." Other group members begin to take sides with either Lise or Midge.

What You Can Do

Defining problems clearly often requires going beyond the team for information. You might say, "I think we're stuck. We have two different opinions about this. Maybe we should ask some other people for their thoughts on this. Who might know more about this kind of situation than we do?"

Lise and Midge contact three curators whose institutions have held an exhibit at the same time another institution has held an exhibit of a well-known figure in the art world. All three say attendance at their exhibits was higher than expected. People who came from out of town for the major exhibit made the rounds of other art exhibits and shows in the area. Kate remains unconvinced.

What You Can Do

You might say, "Kate, I think the team is ready to make a decision on this. We usually vote and go with the majority. Since this is really important to you, I think it would be best in this case to try to reach consensus on this decision. Let's discuss all the options again and see if we can come up with a decision that everyone can live with. Is that OK with everybody?"

By suggesting a change in the decision-making process, you are making it clear to everyone that Kate's position has to be taken seriously. You are also reminding Kate that the team cares about her and also must take action on this issue. Consensus, in this team, doesn't mean that everyone has to be enthusiastic about a decision. It simply means that everyone can live with the decision. After further discussion, Kate may still be skeptical, but she may be willing to go along with the emerging consensus. She may agree to go along this time as an experiment. It is unlikely that Kate will attempt to block the decision. This team has established a norm that encourages members to go along with decisions as long as the team has done its best to discuss the problem, uncover relevant information, and seek input from all members.

Cohesion and Conflict

Positive relationships are evident in high performance teams. Conflicts continue to occur as well. In high performance teams, the following characteristics are evident:

- The team is highly cohesive.
- Interpersonal attraction among members is high.
- Members are cooperative.
- Periods of conflict are frequent but brief.
- The team has effective conflict management strategies.

Some examples of how teams remain cohesive and deal with conflict are provided next.

The team has been thrown a curve ball. The court date has been moved up due to political pressure, and this legal defense team must be prepared for trial much earlier than expected. Members of the team know there's no chance of getting the date moved back. They'll just have to be ready.

What You Can Do

You might say something like, "I was planning to go away for the weekend, but I'll cancel that. That will give me time to work with Janice on preparing those motions. What do you say, Janice?"

Teams at Stage 4 step up to challenges. The world is not predictable. What's more, it is often stressful. In teams that are functioning well, people make the necessary adjustments to get the job done. A word of caution is in order here. If members frequently find themselves in situations like this, it may be a sign that they should review their operational procedures. Too many situations like this one may overload team members and cause burnout. This particular situation seems unavoidable. Others, however, may be avoidable with some forethought.

Bob is getting hot under the collar. He disagrees strongly with Tom's proposed changes in patient education procedures for the unit. "Sure, these changes will save time, but I will not compromise patient care for anybody." Tom is hurt by this statement and says, "I'm not trying to do that. I'm just trying to standardize our approach to patient education. That's what will save the time."

What You Can Do

You know that conflicts occur at every stage of group development. In fact, conflicts are good since they often help to clarify things. You also know that the way conflicts are handled is critical. So, you say, "This is a very important issue. I think we should take both these points of view very seriously and get other members' opinions as well. In fact, it might be useful to see what other units like ours are doing about patient education. What do the rest of you think?"

By redirecting the conversation away from Bob and Tom and back to the team as a whole, tempers will undoubtedly cool. Both men's concerns have been acknowledged and taken seriously. Other members will have the opportunity to weigh in on these issues, and the idea of seeking information from other hospitals will probably be received positively by team members. The trick in conflict situations is to intervene quickly and stay focused on the task.

Maintaining High Performance

High performance is maintained in Stage 4 in the following ways:

- The team gets, gives, and utilizes feedback about its effectiveness and productivity.
- The team evaluates its performance on a regular basis.
- The team takes steps to avoid routine and getting stuck in a rut.

Some examples of how teams maintain high performance and what you can do to help are provided next.

John is facilitating this meeting. The team rotates the job of meeting facilitator, which gives Joyce, the designated leader, the chance to participate more fully in discussions. Halfway through the meeting, John says, "It's time to do a process check."

What You Can Do

This is a simple one. Because you know it's important to evaluate team processes regularly, go along with John's suggestion. There are three ways to evaluate how a team is doing. The first way, which John has suggested, is to take five minutes in the middle of a meeting to answer the following questions:

1. Are we on task and on schedule in terms of covering the agenda?

2. Does everyone feel that he or she has been heard?

3. Does anything need clarification at this point?

4. Is there anything we could do at this point to improve our process?

Taking the time to do a quick evaluation halfway through the meeting is called a process check. Process checks make it possible to correct things that are not going well during the meeting so that changes can be made right away. This prevents the team from spending time unproductively.

Bill, the group leader, says, "At the next meeting, we're scheduled to do a periodic review of how the team is doing. Take the next few minutes to fill out the checklist. Patrick has volunteered to summarize the results for us and to present the summary at the next meeting."

What You Can Do

This one is easy, too. Go along with Bill's suggestion. Respond to the checklist as honestly as possible. The second way to ensure continuous evaluation is to do periodic reviews of team function as Bill has suggested. The length of time between reviews will vary for each team. In general, once every six to eight weeks seems reasonable. The idea is to avoid long periods of lowered productivity by making any necessary changes as soon as possible.

At the end of this chapter, I introduce the Team Performance Checklist. Every six to eight weeks, all members and the leader should take a few minutes at the end of a meeting to complete the checklist. One member should be asked to organize the responses and present the results at the next meeting. The best way to organize the responses is to determine the average response to each question and the average total response.

Begin the next meeting by going over the responses. Look at items where the average response is high (3 or 4). These are things that the team is doing well. Keep doing those things. Next look at items where the average response is low (1 or 2). Discuss strategies to improve the team's performance in those areas. Implement those strategies immediately. Don't forget to check up on yourselves. Do another evaluation about two months later. Repeat the process just described and make any necessary changes.

To some readers, this may seem like a waste of time. It's not. The dynamics of groups and teams can shift quickly. Before you know it, regression to earlier stages has occurred. Teams do not operate in a vacuum. Changes in the external environment can take their toll on the best teams. Budget cuts, downsizing, shifts in organizational priorities, and many other things can affect internal team functioning. Stage 4 teams are not immune to these things. They do have a better chance of surviving these pressures than groups at lower developmental levels do, but only if they are vigilant.

Internal forces can also affect team dynamics. Work pressures, new members, conflicts that arise, and lots of other things can turn a silk purse into a sow's ear. Getting to the top of the development ladder is hard. Staying there is just as hard.

Oscar is worried that the team is not getting enough feedback about its performance from others outside the team. He says, "I think we should try to figure out ways to get better and more regular feedback from others in the organization. We get so caught up in doing the work that we don't take the time to find out what others think of the quality of that work. Can we make that an agenda item at our next meeting?"

What You Can Do

Support Oscar's effort to get the team to discuss ways to get feedback. The third way to evaluate team effectiveness and productivity requires feedback from sources outside the team. Some teams get constant feedback about their performance. Others get almost none. All teams need to figure out ways to determine whether they are meeting goals and whether others are satisfied with their progress and output. Without feedback, it's impossible to know how to improve.

The type of feedback and methods to get that feedback will vary from team to team. The ease or difficulty of devising methods to obtain that feedback will as well. If the team's goals are concrete, it will be easier. If goals are more abstract, it will be harder. For example, if the goal of the team is to increase the number of cars produced in a quarter, feedback is easy to obtain. On the other hand, if the task of the team is to improve, or change, the corporate climate, obtaining timely feedback will be more difficult. Whether feedback is difficult or easy to obtain, without it the team is flying blind. Figure out ways to obtain performance feedback on a regular basis.

By the way, although I've included these evaluation strategies in a discussion of Stage 4 teams, assessing group progress and obtaining performance feedback is necessary at every stage of development. Do it early and often throughout the life span of your group.

Jane says, "I've been feeling a little flat at meetings for the past month. Are we getting a little dull? We were such pistols for quite a while, but I think we're starting to bore each other a little. Is there something we can do to spice things up?"

What You Can Do

My colleagues and I have been doing research on work teams for years. One of the things we've noticed is that teams tend to experience process losses as they age. We've noticed that after about 18 to 24 months, teams that were working at high levels start to falter. Productivity and effectiveness begin to decrease. No one is sure why this happens, but I think it may be the result of fatigue. Team members simply get tired of doing the same old things in the same old way even when those things have been effective. After all the work that goes into creating a high performance team, members tire of it. They want something new and different.

This is not surprising. Human beings tend to be a bit perverse in this regard. After spending years renovating the house, the occupants tire of the decor. After years of living somewhere, some people feel the urge to move. After we've eaten a salad for lunch every day for months, the thought of another salad bores us to tears. We long for stability, and when we achieve it we want something different and challenging.

Teams are composed of humans, and so the urge for novelty and change influences team members. When things become too routine, most of us want change. Our attention goes to other things and away from maintaining high levels of performance.

Again, this is as natural as can be, but, from a work perspective, it may have negative consequences. If the work of the team is completed, it might be best to disband and to distribute the now-routine tasks to others. If the work is not complete, however, team members will need to think of ways to revitalize themselves. Some ways to do this follow:

- Add additional goals and interesting tasks for the team to work on.
- Hold a retreat focused on ways to revitalize team members.
- Switch roles around so that members are doing new and different things.
- Teach one another new aspects of the work.
- Rotate some members off the team and add new members.
- Change the way meetings are conducted.
- Change the meeting time.
- Do other creative things to energize the process.

Stage 4 is the best of times. Do whatever it takes to ensure that "the best of times" doesn't become "the good old days."

Team Performance Checklist

Please read the statements below. Circle the number that most accurately describes your response to the statement. Use the following key to respond to each statement.

1 = disagree strongly

2 = disagree to some extent

3 = agree to some extent

4 = agree strongly

1. Members are clear about group goals.

    1   2   3   4

2. Members agree with group goals.

    1   2   3   4

3. Group tasks require us to work together.

    1   2   3   4

4. Members are clear about their roles.

    1   2   3   4

5. Members accept their roles.

    1   2   3   4

6. Members' assignments match their abilities.

    1   2   3   4

7. The group leader's style changes when necessary to meet emerging group needs.

    1   2   3   4

8. The group has an open communication structure that allows all members to participate.

    1   2   3   4

9. The group gets regular feedback about its productivity.

    1   2   3   4

(Continued)

(Continued)

---

10. Members give each other constructive feedback.

               1   2   3   4

11. The group utilizes feedback about its effectiveness to make improvements in how it is functioning.

               1   2   3   4

12. The group spends time defining and discussing problems it must solve.

               1   2   3   4

13. Members spend time planning how they will solve problems and make decisions.

               1   2   3   4

14. The group uses effective decision-making strategies.

               1   2   3   4

15. The group implements its solutions and decisions.

               1   2   3   4

16. The group develops methods to evaluate its solutions and decisions.

               1   2   3   4

17. The group accepts members who behave differently as long as their behavior is perceived as helpful to task accomplishment.

               1   2   3   4

18. Group norms encourage high performance, quality, and success.

               1   2   3   4

19. Group norms encourage innovative solutions.

               1   2   3   4

20. Subgroups are accepted and integrated into the group as a whole.

               1   2   3   4

21. The group contains the smallest number of members necessary to accomplish its goals.

               1   2   3   4

22. The group has been given sufficient time to develop a mature working unit and to accomplish its goals.

               1   2   3   4

23. The group is highly cohesive and cooperative.

              1   2   3   4

24. Periods of conflict are frequent but brief.

              1   2   3   4

25. The group uses effective conflict management strategies.

              1   2   3   4

Minimum Score: 25

Maximum Score: 100

Your Group's Average Score: _____

What Is Your Group's Stage of Development?

Total Score	Group's Stage
85+	4
70–84	3
<70	1* or 2**

*The group is in Stage 1 if members are tentative, polite, and somewhat passive.

**The group is in Stage 2 if members are disagreeing with each other and/or the leader.

SEVEN

HOW DO HIGH PERFORMANCE TEAMS FUNCTION?

—•◆•—

Some people I've come across think all this focus on team development is a waste of time. They ask if any of this effort makes a difference to the bottom line. They are usually very surprised when I tell them that it does. For example, work teams functioning at the higher stages of group development finish projects faster, produce products of higher quality, and generate more revenue than groups functioning at the lower stages of group development. Students taught by faculty teams functioning at the higher stages of group development score higher on standardized tests. Intensive care staff teams functioning at higher stages of group development save more lives. Paying attention to group development is the key to successful outcomes.

People are right to be skeptical about many of the things currently being done to increase team effectiveness and productivity. Many of them actually are a waste of time. However, some of the things high performance teams do make a very real difference to the bottom line.

Research studies on the relationship between internal team processes and productivity have identified a number of characteristics of high performance teams that are associated with productivity. They are listed next.

The Characteristics of High Performance Teams

1. Members are clear about and agree with the team's goals.

2. Tasks are appropriate to team versus individual solution.

3. Members are clear about and accept their roles.

4. Role assignments match members' abilities.

5. The leadership style matches the team's development level.

6. An open communication structure allows all members to participate.

7. The team gets, gives, and utilizes feedback about its effectiveness and productivity.

8. The team spends time defining and discussing problems it must solve or decisions it must make.

9. Members also spend time planning how they will solve problems and make decisions.

10. The team uses effective decision-making strategies.

11. The team implements and evaluates its solutions and decisions.

12. Task-related deviance is tolerated.

13. Team norms encourage high performance, quality, success, and innovation.

14. Subgroups are integrated into the team as a whole.

15. The team contains the smallest number of members necessary to accomplish its goals.

16. Team members have sufficient time together to develop a mature working unit and to accomplish the team's goals.

17. The team is highly cohesive and cooperative.

18. Periods of conflict are frequent but brief, and the group has effective conflict management strategies.

BOX 7.1   Education Matters

Faculty groups at higher stages of group development have a significantly higher percentage of students who pass proficiency tests than faculty groups at lower stages of group development.

10 Keys to Productivity

The previous list of characteristics of high performance teams suggests that there are 10 key areas members should pay attention to in order to ensure the productivity of their group: goals; roles; interdependence; leadership; communication and feedback; discussion, decision making, and planning; implementation and evaluation; norms and individual differences; structure; and cooperation and conflict management. Each of these areas is discussed next.

Goals

The most important characteristic of a high performance team is that its *members are clear about the team's goals.* Although this seems obvious, I have seen too many groups in which that was not the case. Even if all group members seem to know what the goals are, they often have different ideas about what accomplishing them requires. Even if people are saying the same words, those words may mean different things to different people. For example, I remember a group that was established to develop a strategic plan for a division of a large organization. Each member knew what the goal was, but there were different opinions about what developing a strategic plan actually meant. For some, developing a strategic plan meant engaging in a lengthy process of data collection from organization members, competitors, and customers; reading literature about the industry; and making predictions of future trends in that industry. Once that information was collected and analyzed, they would devise a decision-making process that involved members and customers. Finally, after this lengthy process, they would formulate a strategic plan.

Others in the group had a very different view of what it meant to develop a strategic plan. For them, it meant holding two or three committee meetings, discussing ideas about what the division should do over the next five years, and writing up the ideas that the majority of committee members agreed with.

This example underscores the necessity of thoroughly discussing group goals and what those goals mean to different group members. Until everyone is clear about the goals, it makes no sense to try to work to accomplish them.

Even after everyone is clear about the group's goals, it doesn't necessarily follow that everyone agrees with the goals. One of the characteristics of high performance teams, however, is that *members agree with the team's goals.* This means they think the goals are important, reasonable, and attainable and will benefit the team as well as the organization.

I don't mean to imply people must think every group goal is the best thing since sliced bread or the most exciting assignment they've ever been given. Some goals (cutting the budget, reducing overhead, changing the shipping schedule) are not very exciting but may be important to the team and the organization. The point is that members need to see the relevance of the goals for the team to be successful.

Roles

Once group members have clarified the group's goals and agree on them, the members can begin to organize themselves to accomplish those goals. This usually includes deciding what needs to be done and who should do what in order to achieve the goals.

Using the previous example as a case in point, let's imagine group members agreed that the tasks involved in developing a strategic plan were as follows:

1. Collecting data from organization members

2. Collecting data from competitors

3. Collecting data from customers

4. Reading literature about the current state of the industry

5. Reading literature about future trends in the industry

6. Analyzing the data

7. Developing a decision-making process involving organization members and customers

After lengthy discussions about how each of these tasks might be accomplished, decisions about which member or members should work on each task need to be made. Often, people volunteer to take on certain tasks or the group leader assigns them to tasks. Neither of these options is inherently good or bad. Three things are crucial, however. First, *each member must be clear about the role she or he is being asked to play.* That is, the expectations are clear, and the process for accomplishing the assigned task is clear as well. Second, *each member must have the ability and skills necessary to accomplish the assigned or chosen task.* Third, *each member must agree with and accept the assigned role.*

Again, these requirements for assigning roles seem obvious. In reality, however, it's a rare group that meets these requirements. There are many reasons for this failure to ensure that members are clear about the roles they have been assigned, are able to accomplish them, and are willing to take them on. Here are just a few examples of how good people set themselves up to fail:

- Mary volunteers to collect data from organization members. She is new to the company and doesn't know too many people yet. She has worked for three competitors and would be more valuable in helping to collect information about competitors. Since she volunteered, however, no one is willing to raise any of these issues.

- Joe volunteers to review the literature regarding current and future trends in the industry. He is not computer literate, however, and much of the information will have to be gathered through online databases and the Internet. Again, since he volunteered, no one raises these concerns.

- The group's leader, John, volunteers to analyze the data as it comes in. Sarah is a statistician and would be perfect for this job, but because John is the leader, no one questions his right to assign himself the task.

Interdependence

In successful teams, *tasks require team members to work together* as a unit and in subgroups. In the case of a team developing a strategic plan, since the amount of work involved to reach that goal is well beyond the scope of a single individual, members need to work together as a unit and in subgroups. In addition, the goal requires interdependence, because a strategic plan developed by one person is not likely to reflect the division accurately. A successful strategic plan is one that works. The team working to create such a plan needs to incorporate many viewpoints, accurately interpret and sift through those differing views, and develop a plan that is acceptable to others and will lead the division in a positive direction. This is one of the best reasons for using a group rather than an individual to accomplish certain goals. A well-functioning team will beat an individual in accomplishing this type of goal any day.

Leadership

In productive teams, *the leader's style changes when necessary to meet emerging group needs.* Members' perceptions of the role of the leader also change at different stages of group development. At Stage 1, group members perceive the leader as benevolent and powerful. He or she is perceived as the source of members' safety and reward. At this stage, members expect the leader to be directive. At Stage 2, however, members begin to challenge the leader's authority and control. For the group to mature, such challenges are necessary. The role of the leader must be redefined if the group is to move into the more mature stages of development. Stage 2 leaders should remain directive and gradually begin to involve members in discussing options and exploring issues. By the time a group has reached the third stage of development, group members have assumed many of the roles that were initially the domain of the leader. Finally, at Stage 4, effective leaders act like expert members. Most of the leader's functions have been distributed among team members.

In high performance teams, members assume many of the functions leaders performed at earlier stages. For this to occur, the leader's role must become less directive and more consultative. The leader can help to redistribute power among members by altering her or his leadership style to match the needs of the group. This requires that the leader know what the needs of the group are at any given time and how to behave to facilitate movement. If a leader maintains one style of leadership throughout the life of a group, she or he will not meet group needs and will not facilitate the development of a high performance team. More information about effective leadership can be found in Chapter 9.

Communication and Feedback

High performance teams have an open communication structure that allows all members to participate. Individuals are heard regardless of their age, title, sex, race, ethnicity, profession, and other status characteristics. This enhances productivity because all ideas and suggestions get attention.

High performance teams get regular feedback about their effectiveness and productivity. When members are asked to assess the team's effectiveness and productivity, they are able to answer accurately. This means that members seek feedback about how the team is performing from each other and from external sources.

Members of high performance teams give each other constructive feedback about individual performance and contributions. Constructive feedback promotes improvement and individual development. That is, the feedback is intended to be helpful to the team by improving members' efforts to accomplish goals. It is also intended to be helpful to the individual by providing information he or she can use to become a more effective team member. If feedback does not meet both these criteria, it should not be given.

Finally, *high performance teams utilize feedback about team processes and productivity to make improvements in how they are functioning.* You'd be surprised at the number of groups I've encountered whose members receive feedback about group performance but don't use that feedback to implement constructive changes. In most cases, this is due to a simple flaw in the group's internal processes. Groups that don't utilize feedback constructively usually don't have a mechanism in place to evaluate the validity of the feedback and to make decisions about what changes they should make based on that feedback. An example of such a mechanism might be that internal and external feedback is sought on a regular basis and that the feedback is discussed and evaluated at the beginning of the next meeting. If the feedback is judged to be valid and helpful, members discuss ways to improve team performance, decide what changes to make, and implement those changes.

This may seem like an elaborate process, but in reality it usually takes 10 minutes or less. The trick is to collect the feedback from members at the end of one session and discuss it at the beginning of the next. Feedback from external sources should be collected between meetings.

Discussion, Decision Making, and Planning

High performance teams spend time planning how they will solve problems and make decisions. That is, they determine how decisions will be made before they attempt to make decisions. They may decide that majority vote, a two-thirds majority vote, consensus, or another decision-making strategy will be employed. The key is that these determinations are made in advance and that *the team's decision-making strategy is effective* and meets with member approval.

Also, *high performance teams spend time defining and discussing problems they must solve.* That is, in advance of a final decision, sufficient discussion has occurred so that everyone is clear about the issues involved and the alternative ways of dealing with those issues. If insufficient time is spent in discussion before a decision is made, the resulting decision may be inadequate or in error.

Implementation and Evaluation

High performance teams implement the solutions and decisions made by members. That is, members and the leader follow up on those decisions and hold each other accountable for acting on those decisions. Teams that are successful also develop methods to evaluate team solutions and decisions. Decisions may turn out to be in error or inadequate, but in effective teams, those errors and inadequacies are caught and corrected quickly

Norms and Individual Differences

Successful teams establish norms that encourage high performance, quality, and success. Such teams also have norms that encourage members to be creative and innovative. It would be difficult, if not impossible, for a team to be successful if its members were not expected to perform at high levels.

Another interesting characteristic of effective teams is that *members who behave differently are accepted as long as their behavior is perceived as helpful to task accomplishment.* For example, if a member does not talk as much as other members expect, that member will be accepted as long as the contributions he or she does make are considered helpful. A member who seems loud or a bit aggressive will also be accepted if his or her task-related performance is perceived as useful. In short, successful teams contain members who tolerate, or even enjoy, one another's idiosyncrasies in order to get the job done.

Structure

Three factors are important to the structure of successful teams. First, *successful teams contain the smallest number of members necessary* to accomplish goals and tasks. In a recent study, I investigated 329 work groups to determine whether the size of these groups influenced productivity. The results were quite clear. Groups containing three to six members were significantly more productive than larger groups. Second, the hallmark of a mature team is that *members are able to form subgroups* in order to get work done. Third, subgroups are not perceived as threatening by members who are not part of these groups. Instead, *subgroups are accepted and valued for their contribution to the team.* Subgroups are not seen as renegade or revolutionary groups. Rather, subgroups are integrated into the team as a whole. In short, productive teams are organized. In addition, these *teams have sufficient time together,* overall and at each meeting, to develop and maintain high performance and to accomplish goals.

This last point is worth emphasizing. Most groups need at least eight or nine months together to be successful. I base this time estimate on the research I described earlier that suggests it takes at least six months for a group to mature fully. The length of individual meetings will vary with the complexity of the group's goals. Many meetings simply are too short, however. The most tragic examples of this in my experience come, unfortunately, from my work with schools. Elementary, middle, and high school teachers are expected to deal with complicated responsibilities, include coordinating the curriculum, developing interdisciplinary lesson plans, and monitoring the behavior and progress of students taught by a number of faculty, to name a few. In general, the faculty of a school meets as a whole group once a month or less and for about an hour or so. Faculty subgroups (e.g., seventh-grade teachers) meet more frequently. These subgroups usually meet for 45 minutes once a week. Of course, 45 minutes is actually 30 or 35 minutes because teachers need time to dismiss their students and settle into the meeting. Teachers also have to leave before the end of the allotted time to get to their next class on time, making it difficult to have meaningful and thorough discussion, planning, and decision making.

Each group will have to judge for itself how much time it needs to accomplish its goals and what the length of each meeting should be. It's important that a group not shortchange itself or set itself up for failure by not allowing enough time or by using time inefficiently. Individual members and subgroups can do many tasks between meetings.

Cooperation and Conflict Management

A large body of research confirms that *a high performance team is highly cohesive and contains cooperative members.* Of course, cooperation alone is insufficient to achieve success. The other factors outlined in this chapter must be in evidence as well. For example, in some groups, members cooperate to avoid work. In others, members cooperate to do the minimum amount of work. Clearly, cooperation is not enough, but without it success is very unlikely.

That members cooperate doesn't mean conflict never occurs. In fact, research tells us that productive teams have frequent, but brief, periods of task conflict. Task conflicts are brief because high performance teams have effective conflict management strategies.

Productive teams operate differently from unproductive groups. Productivity is not an accident or the result of one or two people. The way a group functions, from the beginning, does make a difference in its productivity. Studies have found that high performance teams actually produce more than other work groups. Their managers as well as their members rate them as more productive. These studies have been conducted in the financial industry, the hotel industry, the manufacturing sector, the service sector, the healthcare industry, and educational institutions.

It's not a waste of time to pay attention to how your group is functioning. Based on what we now know, it's clear that time spent on increasing the functioning of your group is time well spent. It might be helpful for your group to review the characteristics of high performance teams and determine what your group is doing well and what needs improvement. Use the Team Performance Checklist at the end of Chapter 6 to assess your group's current level of effectiveness. Collate members' responses to questions and determine the group's average score. If that score is 85 or above, you can legitimately call yourselves members of a high performance team. Regardless of the score, there will be areas that need improvement. Plan ways to make necessary adjustments.

∗ EIGHT ∗

EFFECTIVE TEAM MEMBERS

———•═•═•———

S o much has been written about leaders that it would take at least one large library to house all the books, journals, magazines, and other materials that focus on leadership. Materials that focus on membership still fit neatly in a corner on my desk. Leadership training abounds. In all likelihood, dear reader, you have attended leadership training at some point in your career. But have you been to membership training? Sadly, I think your answer would be no. Have you ever seen a brochure or ad in a professional journal that describes a membership training workshop? I haven't, and advertisements for training cross my desk almost every day. Besides, who wants to go to membership training? It would be like volunteering for a remedial class in high school. Winners go to leadership training. Only losers need to learn how to be effective members.

Of course, nothing could be further from the truth. Unless all members work to ensure group success, it won't happen. Leaders and members all have to put their oars in the water and row in the same direction to reach the group's goals. No one gets to be a bystander in the process of group development.

Actually, I'm getting tired of writing about the lack of work group membership training. The first edition of *Creating Effective Teams* was published in 1999. It's now 2012 and I'm working on the fourth edition but nothing much has changed in the membership training department. Membership training has not caught on. It's not fair to ask people to participate in a group at work without helping them acquire the skills they need to be effective members. For my part, I no longer offer leadership training. Instead, I train work groups in effective membership and effective leadership. Members and leaders of real work groups learn together and learn each other's roles. This approach is much more fruitful since the attitudes and skills participants acquire can be put to use at the group's next meeting. Also, members and the leader can help each other become more productive by supporting each other and offering advice.

This chapter outlines what research tells us about the behaviors and attitudes of effective team members. They are presented in the form of guidelines. None of these characteristics requires any special personality type, but they all require good will and some degree of effort. As you read through the chapter, think about a group you are working with at the moment. Ask yourself the following questions:

- Do I follow these guidelines?
- Can I think of times when I exhibited these behaviors and attitudes?
- Can I think of times when I should have exhibited these behaviors but, for some reason, did not?
- In what areas do I need to improve?
- What do I plan to do to improve in these areas?

If you're going to be an effective team member, you'll need to take a closer look at your own behaviors and attitudes and at the way you interact with the group. Here are some guidelines to help you evaluate your performance as a group member.

Don't blame others for group problems.

One of the more difficult issues I frequently encounter in working with groups is a general feeling of helplessness that individuals express. Somehow, members of groups are convinced that they can't make a difference when it comes to success. I hear lots of statements like the following:

"Unless the leader is replaced, there's nothing the rest of us can do."

"These people are crazy. I don't even want to come to meetings."

"Team meetings are like swimming with sharks. I just keep my head down."

"Our meetings are a waste of time. I wish the leader were stronger."

"I'm not even sure what we're supposed to be doing, but I'm afraid to ask."

"The same people talk in circles. I just keep quiet and hope the meeting will end soon."

"There's nothing we can do. Upper management has to get into the act before things will change."

I encounter these feelings of helplessness very often among people in the workplace. Of course, I realize that things can be pretty chaotic in organizations because of downsizing, mergers, new initiatives, recessions, and the like, but I am not convinced that those are the only reasons for the passivity I observe. One reason is the human tendency to blame the other guy.

It will probably surprise many readers to learn that there's a social science term that describes this tendency to blame the other guy. It's called the *fundamental attribution error.* What it means is that humans have a tendency to attribute the actions of others to personality characteristics without taking other factors into account. Most of the time that's an error.

Our tendency to blame the boss for poor group results without taking budgetary constraints, the lack of group member cooperation, or the lack of other necessary resources into account is an example of an attribution error. When we say lack of upper management support is the reason for group failure, despite the fact that many group members don't even come to meetings and no one can agree when they do come, that's an attribution error. When members say Harry is at fault because he just won't shut up despite the fact that no one else seems willing to talk, that's an attribution error.

Researchers have also uncovered some general patterns in how individual group members interpret group success or failure. For example, leaders and powerful members tend to feel personally responsible for both group success and group failure. Members in general, on the other hand, take responsibility for group success but not for group failure. Instead, these members attribute group failure to leaders, powerful members, the organization, upper management, or other situational constraints.

People tend to misinterpret the behavior and motivation of others. This tendency to misinterpret increases conflict situations. So, when things aren't going well for the group, we are much more likely to blame others for the situation. While the tendency to misjudge people, events, and actions is natural, it also has very negative effects on the group and on individuals who are wrongly judged.

For example, I am often called upon to assist work groups that are mired in conflict and, as a result, are not within budget or time constraints or are not meeting target goals. There is usually a stable behavior pattern of attacks and counterattacks that has been going on for some time. My goal in work-ing with such a group is to help the group free itself from this pattern and get back on track.

The problem confronting me in such a situation is that, because the group is stuck in a pattern of conflict, members tend to be focused on blaming out-side forces, other members, or the leader for the group's predicament. As long as blaming is the primary pattern, the group will remain stuck. Also, the longer the blaming continues, the more powerless and frustrated group mem-bers will feel.

Changing a pattern of blame to one of collaboration and shared responsi-bility for group functioning and productivity, however, is no easy task. Schein, a well-known organizational consultant, wrote that the concept of teamwork is inconsistent with the U.S. emphasis on individualism and personal responsi-bility. Consequently, if members accept shared responsibility for group func-tion, each member will feel compelled to accept personal blame for group failure as well. Resistance to any information that disconfirms the belief that the group's problems are due to the actions of an individual member, the leader, or authority figures external to the group is the inevitable result. Unless group members begin to see the situation differently, no change will occur.

One of the most powerful ways I have found to help members change their view of the situation is to talk with them about the normal human ten-dency to blame the other guy. Once members realize they have made a mis-take, they begin to look for other factors that are inhibiting progress. From that point on, changes happen fairly rapidly. Simply put, blaming is a symptom of a negative group pattern. Blaming is almost never a statement of fact. It is rare that one person is responsible for a group's problems. I believe it best to assume this is never the case, because that stops the blaming, which often leads the group in a positive direction.

Since I've heard it so many times before, I can almost hear some readers saying that, in their case, the leader really was to blame. Others are thinking it really was that member Harry's fault. Still others are thinking that upper man-agement really was to blame.

I hear these statements so often it seems as if every leader, on every con-tinent, is incompetent. I hear these statements so frequently that it seems as if every group, on every continent, contains an incompetent, evil, or mentally unbalanced member. This is simply not the case. Most groups contain people who are trying to do a good job. They may not know how. They may not be socially skilled, but they are trying.

My advice is to give everyone the benefit of the doubt not just for his or her sake but for your own and the group's sake. Blaming doesn't help. It only starts cycles of revenge and retaliation. Instead, find other factors that might be blocking group progress and fix them. Use some of the checklists in this book to help you determine other things to focus on. You'll be surprised at what happens when you do that. Things will start to get better.

By the way, I want to encourage people in management roles to start taking this advice as well. Stop replacing leaders or group members for alleged incompetence. Give teams the resources and training they need to work together effectively. Supply consultants if necessary. All of us can make attribution errors, and the human cost for these errors is very high.

I have two reasons for starting this chapter by introducing you to the human tendency to blame the other guy. First, it has pained me to repeatedly witness these misjudgments and their aftermath (e.g., transfers, firings, hurt feelings, and stress). Second, this is a pretty direct way of saying that all group members and leaders have responsibility for group success and group failings. The rest of the organization does, as well. Chapter 10 will outline what we know from research about what organizations can do to help the groups functioning within them. Chapter 9 will outline what leaders can do to help their groups be successful. This chapter outlines what members can do to help their group be successful. Everybody shares in the responsibility, and that's the truth.

Encourage the process of goal, role, and task clarification.

Encouraging the process of goal, role, and task clarification is simple. All it means is that when you don't understand what's going on, ask questions until you do. It helps to ask questions of the group and not just the leader, because the discussion that follows will be richer and more likely to really clarify things for everyone.

While this is a very simple thing to do, people hesitate to ask questions in the early stages of group development. This reticence is quite natural, but try to overcome it a little. Even if you ask only one question of the group, it will make a difference.

Many people have told me they are afraid to ask questions for fear of being perceived as incompetent or naive. I am quite aware that image is considered important at work, but image isn't everything. Even if image is very important, asking clarifying questions is unlikely to hurt your image. In fact, it may improve it. Others are most likely to see you as helpful, courageous, or down to earth for asking clarifying questions. None of those qualities is bad for your image.

Encourage the adoption of an open communication structure where all member input and feedback is heard.

It won't come as a surprise to most readers that some people talk more than others during meetings. Of course, some people are just shy or have less need to be heard than others do. Many, however, talk less because they don't feel invited to speak. This has happened to most of us at one time or another. You go to the first meeting of a group and few people talk to you. When you do say something, very few people respond to what you've said. Think about the kind of group that was and the kind of people it contained. Was there anything about you that was different from others? Were you:

- One of the oldest in the group?
- One of the youngest in the group?
- New to the organization or group?
- One of only a few women in an otherwise male group?
- One of only a few men in an otherwise female group?
- The only one from your profession or area?
- One of only a few minorities in the group?

Were there any other obvious differences between you and other group members?

People tend unconsciously to classify others and assign high or low status to them based on external characteristics, especially during early meetings. Things as seemingly meaningless as height, clothes, mannerisms, and the like sometimes get you classified into a high- or low-status position in a group.

By the way, people aren't bad when they classify others and assign them high or low status based on that classification. We all do it, all the time, sometimes without even being aware of what we're doing. In some cases, our tendency to do this can be very helpful. It can keep us out of harm's way. In work groups, however, our tendency to do this can be quite detrimental.

At the beginning of a group, communication patterns are established very quickly. Who talks to whom and who gets to talk a lot or a little become clear within a few meetings. No one talks about this. It just happens. The problem with this is that who talks to whom and who gets to talk a lot or a little are usually determined by status characteristics such as age, gender, ethnicity, organizational position, and the like. Once you're assigned a position in the food chain, it's hard to break out of it.

Women and minorities, for example, still tend to be assigned lower status in groups. As a result, they are expected to talk less, and they may be assigned less influential group roles. They often report dissatisfaction with their lower status, and other group members sometimes report uncertainty about the status of minority and female group members. While this is changing, we have a long way to go before the tendency to assign lower status to members of certain groups is eradicated.

Group performance suffers when member role and status assignments are inappropriate or when member contributions are ignored. Potentially valuable contributions are overlooked, and goal achievement and productivity suffer as a result. Researchers have identified individual strategies and group conditions, however, that increase the status of women, minorities, and culturally diverse members in groups. These strategies may be helpful to any individual whose group role or status is not commensurate with her or his abilities.

Individuals who do not accept the lower status assigned to them increase the likelihood of improving their position in the group. People who act in group-oriented, as opposed to individually oriented, ways tend to improve their group status as well. Also, people who demonstrate their competence and abilities to the group tend to increase their status, especially if they have enough time to demonstrate that competence. Eventually, other group members see these abilities and it is no longer necessary for the individual to prove his or her worth to the group.

Although research has focused mainly on women and minorities, the same advice works for anyone who is perceived as having a lower status for whatever reason. On the individual level, the research suggests that the following strategies can help to elevate one's status in the group:

- Diplomatically resisting an inappropriate role assignment or status
- Demonstrating one's competence and abilities
- Acting in a cooperative, group-oriented way

On the group level, time aids the process of redefinition or reassignment of roles and changes in communication patterns. There's another factor that helps tremendously. When all members take responsibility to ensure that everyone is heard and that they are all clear about and comfortable with their roles, the chances of group success are heightened. Valuable input and skills will be utilized instead of lost.

Ensuring that everyone has the opportunity to be heard can be as simple as stopping periodically to check in with everyone. This takes only a few minutes but can make a big difference in fostering group success.

Promote an appropriate ratio of task and supportive communications.

In Chapter 2, we discussed the importance of supportive comments to group success. Needless to say, statements focused on the group's work task are very important as well. If we engage only in supportive conversation, we may feel better but won't get much work done. Members of successful work teams spend between 70% and 80% of the time talking about goals and tasks. This means that out of 100 statements made by team members, 70 to 80 will be work oriented. The next most frequent kind of statement made in high performance teams will be supportive. The remainder will be statements that express disagreement, focus on topics unrelated to the task, or express some form of dependency. If the proportion of these various kinds of statements changes very much, the group will be less successful.

What this means in practical terms is that when the group strays into an extended conversation about the football game last night, it would be helpful to try to refocus members on the task at hand. Likewise, if the group has been intensely discussing work tasks for an extended period, it might be helpful to compliment the group for its efforts or, in some other way, express support. Balance in group conversation, as in life, helps a lot.

Promote the use of effective problem-solving and decision-making procedures.

Before I discuss the process of problem solving and decision making, it is necessary to bring up an important question. That is, who should participate in

solving problems and making decisions? Most organizations encourage work-
ers at all levels to participate in these important processes. However, research
suggests that not all employees are capable of contributing to the problem-
solving or decision-making process. Some people simply aren't interested in
these processes, and others don't feel they know enough to help. To solve
problems, group members require expertise in the problem area, confidence in
their ability to help solve the problem, knowledge and experience related to
the problem, interest in participating, and problem-solving process skills.

Effective methods for problem solving and decision making have been
studied by a number of researchers. Their results are, in general, overlapping.
For example, Shaw, a social psychologist, stated that effective group problem
solving and decision making consists of four steps:

- Recognizing the problem
- Diagnosing the problem
- Making the decision
- Accepting and implementing the decision

Others have outlined a process, similar to Shaw's, that includes the
following:

- An orientation phase
- A discussion phase
- A decision phase
- An implementation phase

Each of these phases has significant impact on the quality of a group's
solutions and its overall productivity. For example, during the orientation
phase, it is helpful to avoid dwelling on the problem, since focusing on defi-
ciencies may lead members to become defensive. Instead, it is useful to begin
by discussing solutions that have been effective and investigating solutions
developed by teams in other organizations that have been effective. This puts a
positive spin on the process and may expand the group's solution options. Then
the problem is defined and strategies are outlined for solving the problem.
Strategies include such things as how to gain needed information about the
problem, how to analyze the information, and how to make the final decision.
Research tells us that groups that outline these strategies in advance are more

successful than are those that do not. Unfortunately, many groups spend little or no time planning strategies for problem solving and decision making. Some groups consider it a waste of time, even if members have been made aware of the fact that planning increases solution quality and group performance.

The amount of time spent discussing the problem and potential solutions increases the quality of the outcome. The amount of member participation in the discussion relates to the quality of the group's solution and overall effectiveness as well. Again, many groups don't spend adequate time discussing an issue. In some cases, a group will discuss only a few alternative solutions.

Groups can make the actual decision in a number of ways. The group may delegate the responsibility for the final decision to an individual, a subgroup, or an expert. Member inputs can be averaged to form the basis for a decision. Group members can vote on alternative proposals, or they may choose consensus as their decision-making method. Consensus refers to reaching a decision that is agreeable to all members. Efforts to determine which of these methods is best have been unsuccessful. Individuals like the consensus method, but it doesn't necessarily produce better decisions. In general, people tend to like any method as long as they can live with the final decision. It is certain, however, that participation in the decision-making process does increase member satisfaction. It may also increase performance to some extent.

I want to insert a word of caution regarding the appropriate use of consensus. Many people think consensus means everyone agrees 100% with the proposal. Otherwise, they believe, consensus hasn't been reached. This way of looking at consensus is very dangerous. If one person objects, the group can't move forward. Consensus, viewed in this way, is more like tyranny. One person can stop the group in its tracks. To avoid this pitfall, I recommend a modified version of consensus where members assume consensus exists if 70% or 80% of the members agree. In the last paragraph, I defined consensus as the process of reaching a decision that is agreeable to all members. This doesn't mean all members would rate the proposed solution as their first choice; it simply means all members can live with the decision.

Implementing and evaluating group decisions are key elements in problem solving. Ideally, evaluation is built into the process, and the results of the evaluation form the basis for the group's next problem-solving process. Many of us have sat on committees and made recommendations that were never implemented. This is often the case when the group making the decision doesn't have the authority to implement its solution. Nothing is as demoralizing to a group. It is then incumbent on the group, throughout its deliberations, to interact with other groups that will be involved in implementation. This increases the likelihood of successful implementation of group decisions.

These findings suggest that problem solving and decision making are enhanced when groups outline, in advance, the strategies they will use to solve problems and make decisions. Lengthy discussion of alternative solutions, making sure of implementation and evaluation, and involvement of all members in these processes are also associated with quality problem solving and decision making.

Encourage the establishment of norms that support productivity, innovation, and freedom of expression.

You might be surprised at the number of groups I encounter that don't expect to generate the best possible product or result. I hear what group members feel they can get away with and why time constraints, policies, and lack of resources prohibit the group from doing a good job. It's true that some of these constraints are very real, but if a group agrees to mediocrity, that's what it will get. When groups agree to do the best possible job and to remove as many obstacles from their way as they can, excellence is the likely result.

I addressed freedom of expression earlier when I advocated the development of an open communication structure. If members don't feel free to offer their ideas, it will be difficult for the group to be successful. In this section, I would like to add a few additional comments about freedom of expression.

Research on the effect of diversity in work group procedures and productivity has not led to unanimous conclusions. Some findings suggest that diversity improves work group performance, but other findings conclude that diversity has negative effects on performance. Surface level differences, such as ethnicity, gender, race, and age, have been found to have negative effects on group processes and performance. Underlying differences, such as personality, education, and life experiences, don't have as much impact on work groups. Interpersonal conflicts, however, have very harmful effects on groups. Whether or not those conflicts are instigated by diversity, personality, gender, or the like, these conflicts can have very negative effects on work groups. Sometimes diversity increases interpersonal conflicts. However, diversity can also increase team learning, problem solving, and innovation.

It may be that these contradictions in research findings are due to the significant increases in racial and ethnic diversity not only in the U.S., but also in countries all over the world. Social scientists are capturing glimpses of the rapidly changing makeup of populations across the globe and our efforts to become more inclusive.

In the meantime, what can work group members do to improve group performance and increase the participation of all members? Fortunately, the research is quite clear about one thing: Group members need to avoid interpersonal conflicts and embrace task conflicts. Functional differences among members, such as expertise, background, education level, and the like, lead to task conflicts, which are very helpful and necessary for effective problem solving, decision making, and high performance. If team members focus on the work and avoid interpersonal conflicts, diversity of all types becomes a resource. Members learn from each other, make better decisions, and improve group productivity and effectiveness. To benefit from diversity, everyone must be heard and involved in the discussion.

Go along with norms that promote group effectiveness and productivity.

Norms are collective value judgments about how members should behave and what should be done in the group. Norms are necessary if group members are to coordinate their efforts and accomplish their goals. Establishing rules or norms about unimportant things or the wrong things, however, has a chilling effect on groups. If, for example, individuals cannot express dissent, things will not go well.

Sometimes norms get established about unimportant things. For example, I know of groups in which members are expected to eat lunch together every day. In other groups, members are expected to come to work at least an hour before work actually begins. Norms like these may inhibit individual freedom and cause resentment.

On the other hand, some degree of coordination and conformity is necessary for group success. It is important, then, to go along with norms that promote group effectiveness and productivity. While you might have favored a different way of doing things, if the established norm is likely to work, conformity is advised.

The question that arises at this point is, which norms encourage productivity? Research tells us that norms encouraging high performance standards and effectiveness increase team productivity. Shared expectations of success also support productivity. A norm that encourages innovation increases the likelihood of higher productivity as well. Norms and values that support superior quality, service, innovation, and attention to detail significantly increase team effectiveness and productivity. Make sure your team has norms like these and doesn't create other norms that block effectiveness, and things will go well.

Promote group cohesion and cooperation.

The following are some of the positive effects of cohesion in groups:

- Increased conformity
- Increased group influence over its members
- Increased member satisfaction with the group
- Increased group integration
- Increased cooperation

Cooperation, which is facilitated by cohesion and shared goals, has many positive effects on group functioning. The characteristics of cooperative groups are listed next:

- More effective communication
- A friendlier group atmosphere
- Stronger individual desire to work on group tasks
- Stronger feelings of commitment to the group
- Greater division of labor
- Greater coordination of effort
- Greater productivity
- Increased trust and the development of lasting agreements
- Increased ability to resolve conflicts

A word of caution with regard to cohesion is appropriate at this point. High levels of cohesion, in conjunction with certain factors, can have negative effects. That is, a group can make poor or, in some cases, dangerous decisions due to an overriding wish to maintain unity and cohesion. This wish can lead the group to overlook other choices or courses of action. A group may be in danger of making a poor decision—a condition referred to as "group-think"— if that group is cohesive and also has the characteristics in the situations described next.

- When groups deliberate in relative isolation and do not report, or check, their conclusions with others outside the group, the possibility of poor decisions increases.
- If the group's leader controls the discussion and makes his or her positions clear from the outset, poor group decisions are more likely.
- If the group is faced with a major and stressful decision, the tendency to decide quickly to reduce stress is enhanced. This often results in poor decisions as well.

Cohesion alone does not pose a threat. As long as a group stays connected with others outside the group and has an effective leader, high levels of cohesion will have many positive effects on group productivity. How, then, can group members promote cohesion? Research tells us that when goals and methods to reach those goals are clear, cohesion increases. Also, successful conflict resolution reduces individual fears of rejection and increases trust among members. A feeling of "we-ness," or cohesiveness, results. Finally, while it is rarely clear what causes what in an interacting system, increased communication is associated with increased cohesion and vice versa.

You will notice that the research does not suggest that sharing personal feelings, developing personal friendships, socializing outside of work, and similar things increase group cohesion. It isn't necessary to know other group members on a personal level to promote cohesion. Working to increase goal clarity and communication should occur in the work group. Conflict resolution should as well.

BOX 8.1   Group Therapy?

I got a call from a group leader. He said his group was a mess. When I asked what was happening, he gave me a lengthy personality profile of each group member. He also told me how each person related to other members and who was feuding with whom. The group's problem turned out to be lack of clarity about goals and tasks. When these issues were straightened out, the "personality problems" went away. Psychoanalysis was not necessary.

Conflicts continue to occur throughout a group's life. In fact, group conflict is almost as common as group cooperation. One could assume that conflict seriously impairs group cohesion. While this can be the result, cohesion can also be positively affected by conflict. Although this sounds paradoxical, it is important to note that, in any relationship, the freedom to be oneself and to disagree without fear of rejection or retribution increases, rather than decreases, cohesion and trust. Also, conflict provides energy to the group and allows for clarification of group values, goals, and structures. All of these have been found to be associated with increased cohesion and trust. Cohesion and conflict are linked. You can't have one without the other, so to speak.

Of course, how conflict is dealt with is the crucial factor in determining its effect on cohesion. Inevitably, conflict is resolved. How it is resolved will determine whether group cohesion is positively or negatively affected. Six methods of conflict resolution have been described by a number of researchers:

- Imposition of the position of an individual or subgroup on other members
- Withdrawal of an individual or subgroup from the group
- Inaction, where one or both sides of a conflict do nothing to resolve the conflict
- Yielding, where one side gives up its position
- Compromise, where the parties find a solution somewhere between their respective positions
- Problem solving, where the source of the conflict is located and a mutually agreeable solution is found

The first four solutions have many negative repercussions. Imposition can result in hostility and passive-aggressive behavior on the part of group members. Withdrawal threatens the life of the group and reduces its resources through member loss. Inaction can result in simmering discontent, apathy, or alienation. Yielding may also elicit alienation and covert hostility. Compromise can be viable if the resolution of the conflict seems reasonable and acceptable to all concerned. Problem solving, however, gives the best results because it requires the actual resolution of different perspectives and a new group conceptualization of the issues involved in the conflict.

Some groups navigate their conflicts well, and others disband or become dysfunctional by dealing with their differences ineffectively. What do successful teams do to promote positive conflict resolution? Members of successful teams communicate their views clearly and explicitly. They avoid generalizations and are specific in their communication. They talk about trust and cooperation during the discussion. Members also initially respond cooperatively to others who are behaving competitively. If others continue to respond competitively, successful group members demonstrate their willingness to compete by arguing their position. While this sounds like an inappropriate strategy, research suggests that this may result in cooperation from others, since not to do so would result in continued stress or personal losses. Sometimes, demonstrating a willingness to compete will bring about cooperation from others. Demonstrating a willingness to compete may also result in being viewed as a more formidable opponent.

All of these strategies help maintain a reasonable trust level, which allows negotiations to proceed. Negotiation is an important conflict resolution strategy. Seeking a mutually agreeable, or win-win, solution has been found to increase communication and cooperation. It also tends to reduce the conflict by breaking it down into specific issues that can be dealt with one at a time.

Sometimes the conflict is too deep and intense to be solved by the group members themselves. In such cases, seeking the aid of a third party can help. Group and organizational consultants are often asked to assist groups that are stuck as a result of seemingly insurmountable conflicts. This can be a useful strategy for conflict resolution. However, third-party intervention should be sought only if all parties want the help and if the intensity of the conflict is high. This last-resort strategy requires willingness on the part of the group and considerable skill on the part of the third party.

Interact with others outside the group in ways that promote group integration and cooperation within the larger organizational context.

Ancona, a group researcher, argued that mature, internal group functioning is not enough to ensure group effectiveness. Groups and their members must regularly interact with the rest of the organization to be successful. Groups need support from and information about what is going on in the rest of the organization. Ancona proposed four key external activities that group members should perform. These activities are described next.

Negotiation with other groups and individuals external to the group is necessary to secure needed resources. For example, some group members might be designated to serve on interdepartmental committees or to meet with other groups or individuals in an attempt to influence policies concerning such things as organizational distribution of resources or procedural decisions. Negotiation with other groups is also necessary when conflicts arise.

BOX 8.2   Interspecies Conflict

An organization dedicated to animal welfare reorganized its employees into species-specific teams. Soon after, the Whale team and the Seal team began to fight over resources. The Whale team was accused of throwing its weight around.

Information exchange and scanning involves gathering facts and impressions from other parts of the organization to determine current and future conditions and their potential impact on the group. These activities help the group adapt to the environment and make decisions regarding how to respond to these conditions.

Buffering entails protecting the group from too much external information or pressure. Because too much input can negatively affect internal group processes, buffering is sometimes necessary. One or more members may perform the role of sentry or guard to insulate the group from excessive external demands. If buffering is used as a strategy for too long, however, it may encourage an isolationist stance that will decrease communication with others and reduce the likelihood of group success as a result.

Strategic management and *profile management* involve communicating with external individuals and groups to influence their perceptions of and behaviors toward your group. How a group is perceived by other groups in the organization affects the group by either increasing or decreasing others' willingness to provide resources or to work with that group. Groups can consciously help shape their image by planning what information they will share with others.

Support the leader's efforts to facilitate group goal achievement.

This chapter began with a discussion of the fact that many group members blame the leader for group problems and failures. Effective team members, however, do the opposite. That is, they support the leader's efforts to coordinate and facilitate the group. Effective team members volunteer to perform tasks that need to be done. They also ask questions for clarification, offer advice to the leader when appropriate, and in many other ways actively participate in the leadership function. Group development and effectiveness hinge on the willingness of members to assume some leadership functions and the willingness of leaders to delegate those functions.

The Effective Member Checklist summarizes what has been discussed about effective membership. Spend some time and check yourself. How could you improve? Encourage other group members to do likewise.

Effective Member Checklist

Please read the statements below. Circle the number that most accurately describes your response to the statement. Use the following key to respond to each statement.

1 = disagree strongly

2 = disagree to some extent

3 = agree to some extent

4 = agree strongly

Section I

1. I avoid blaming others for group problems.

        1   2   3   4

2. I assume that every group member is trying to do a good job.

        1   2   3   4

(Continued)

(Continued)

3. I treat people as individuals and don't make assumptions about them based on my preconceived notions about people like them.

        1   2   3   4

4. I do not get bogged down in interpersonal issues or personality conflicts.

        1   2   3   4

Section I Score: _____

Section II

5. I encourage the process of goal, role, and task clarification.

        1   2   3   4

6. I encourage the use of effective problem-solving and decision-making procedures.

        1   2   3   4

7. I encourage the group to outline, in advance, the strategies that will be used to solve problems and make decisions.

        1   2   3   4

8. I work to ensure that decisions and solutions are implemented and evaluated.

        1   2   3   4

9. I encourage norms that support productivity, innovation, and freedom of expression.

        1   2   3   4

10. I encourage the use of effective conflict management strategies.

        1   2   3   4

11. I support division of labor necessary to accomplish goals.

        1   2   3   4

Section II Score: _____

Section III

12. I work to ensure that the input and feedback of every member is heard.

     1   2   3   4

13. I work to ensure that we all have a chance to demonstrate our competence and skills in the group.

     1   2   3   4

14. I discourage any group tendency to adopt excessive or unnecessary norms.

     1   2   3   4

15. I am, and encourage others to be, cooperative.

     1   2   3   4

16. In conflict situations, I communicate my views clearly and explicitly.

     1   2   3   4

17. I respond cooperatively to others who are behaving competitively.

     1   2   3   4

Section III Score: _____

Section IV

18. I act, and encourage others to act, in the best interests of the group.

     1   2   3   4

19. When members contribute good ideas, I express my appreciation.

     1   2   3   4

20. I encourage and work to achieve mutually agreeable solutions to conflict.

     1   2   3   4

21. I support the leader's efforts to coordinate and facilitate group goal achievement.

     1   2   3   4

22. I offer advice to the leader when I think the advice will be helpful.

     1   2   3   4

Section IV Score: _____

(Continued)

(Continued)

Section V

23. I have negotiated, or would be willing to negotiate, with other groups and individuals to help my group obtain needed resources.

    1   2   3   4

24. I share information and impressions I have about other parts of the organization with the group.

    1   2   3   4

25. I encourage the group not to overwhelm itself with too much external information or demands.

    1   2   3   4

26. I talk positively about my group to outsiders.

    1   2   3   4

27. I keep other members of the organization informed about what my group is doing.

    1   2   3   4

Section V Score: _____

Section VI

28. When members stray off the task, I diplomatically try to bring the discussion back to the task.

    1   2   3   4

29. I go along with norms that promote group effectiveness and productivity.

    1   2   3   4

30. I encourage high performance standards.

    1   2   3   4

31. I expect the group to be successful and productive.

    1   2   3   4

32. I encourage innovative ideas.

	1	2	3	4

33. I use what I have learned about group development and productivity to help my group become effective.

	1	2	3	4

34. I encourage the group to frequently assess and alter its functioning, if necessary.

	1	2	3	4

35. I volunteer to perform tasks that need to be done.

	1	2	3	4

Section VI Score: _____

Total Minimum Score: 35
Total Maximum Score: 140

My Score: _____

What Is Your Overall Membership Quotient?

Total Score	Your Membership Grade
126+	A
112–125	B
98–111	C

What Are Your Section Scores?

Section I: Attitudes and Feelings

Total Score	Your Grade
14+	A
12–13	B
10–11	C

(Continued)

(Continued)

Section II: Processes and Procedures

Total Score	Your Grade
25+	A
22–24	B
20–21	C

Section III: Communication and Participation

Total Score	Your Grade
22+	A
19–21	B
16–18	C

Section IV: Support and Encouragement

Total Score	Your Grade
18+	A
16–17	B
14–15	C

Section V: Intergroup Relations

Total Score	Your Grade
18+	A
16–17	B
14–15	C

Section VI: Work and Productivity

Total Score	Your Grade
29+	A
25–28	B
22–24	C

NINE

EFFECTIVE TEAM LEADERSHIP

The belief that leaders are instrumental in the creation of effective teams is deeply rooted in society and in the social sciences. Today's conceptions of leadership are not very different from early views, which described leaders as individuals possessing special inborn characteristics that propelled them into leadership roles. Now, although most social scientists reject the notion of inborn traits, many still see leadership as residing in the individual, because it is assumed that individuals can learn how to be effective leaders by acquiring certain knowledge and skills. Hundreds of thousands of managers and executives have attended leadership training programs over the years in their quest to be effective leaders.

Leaders are thought to facilitate the development of shared understanding and interpretations of reality among group members. They articulate things that have not been explicitly stated before that can provide new visions for the group. Inherent in this position is the assumption that the leadership role is vital to the creation and maintenance of an effective team. This assumption has led some researchers to study the cognitive capacities of leaders in order to determine how effective leaders think about their role. Again, the goal of such studies is to discover effective leadership styles that can be taught to other leaders and potential leaders.

The old notion of the charismatic leader is experiencing a comeback. In this view, the leader is seen as the one who instills new thinking in followers and redirects group activities. These views of leadership support the assumption that leaders are central to the creation and redirection of group culture. In fact, leaders are perceived as having so much power that, should they act in selfish or unethical ways, great damage can be done to the group and its members. Leaders are clearly perceived as capable of making a significant difference in groups.

For the average person in a leadership role in the workplace, these views of leaders as crucial to group success can be overwhelming. It's all up to you when you're the leader. If the group fails, it's your fault. The stress of this enormous personal responsibility can have negative effects on potential or actual leaders. Potential leaders may choose not to become leaders, and actual leaders may suffer emotional or physical stress as a result of this sense of tremendous responsibility.

Some social scientists disagree with this prevailing, relatively one-sided view of the leader as central to team effectiveness and success. Some speak to the interdependence of leaders, followers, and the dynamic forces in which a group is operating. In this view, all group members share the responsibility for the creation of an effective team. Multiple discussions among all members eventually result in shared assumptions about goals and the methods to accomplish those goals. Leaders are part of this process but not necessarily a primary part. Group success or failure is the result of many mutual influences.

Group development theories also suggest that a group's culture and structure are the products of processes inherent in groups. This view of the creation of effective teams is not as leadercentric. The creation of group culture is seen as the result of inherent forces, so the content of culture in different groups is not uniform. Rather, the particulars of a culture result from the resolution of differences and disagreements that emerge in that group. The process, however, is the same from group to group, and all members are involved in the creation of a group's unique culture and structure.

While minority opinions such as those just reviewed do exist, the majority view of leaders as key to group success dominates our thinking. In this chapter, I will try to reduce that domination a bit and alleviate the overwhelming feeling of responsibility associated with leadership in today's work environment. I will present guidelines for leaders regarding what they can do to help their groups become effective and productive teams. These guidelines, like all the others throughout this book, are based on research. Inherent in these guidelines is an assumption of mine, which is that leaders alone cannot be held responsible for group success or failure. Having reviewed the leadership research, I am convinced that the view of groups as interdependent systems is the more accurate one. I have already alluded to this assumption in previous chapters. In fact, two of the preceding chapters could not have been written if I believed leaders were ultimately responsible for group outcomes. The larger organization, external conditions, and group members also influence group success or failure. While leaders can help or hinder the process, so can others.

I also want to dispel the myth that leaders must be special people with a tremendous amount of skill in order to be effective. The average person of goodwill, who is flexible and willing to learn some basic skills, can be an effective leader. Not all situations require leaders of exceptional skill. In fact, in many group situations, charismatic leaders may inhibit group progress because their dominating presence may reduce member participation and motivation to take on certain tasks necessary for group success. Groups work well when all members actively participate. If leaders remain prominent throughout group life, groups will be less likely to succeed. With these assumptions as a foundation, the following guidelines for effective leadership are presented. As you read through the chapter, think about a group you are leading at the moment or have recently led. Ask yourself the following questions:

1. Do I follow these guidelines?
2. Can I think of times when I exhibited these behaviors or attitudes?
3. Can I think of times when I should have exhibited these behaviors or attitudes but, for some reason, did not?
4. In what areas do I need to improve?
5. What do I plan to do to improve in these areas?

There are certain things you must keep in mind and certain things you must do if you are to be an effective team leader. The following guidelines outline how leaders become effective.

Don't take on every leadership assignment you are offered.

Research attempts to determine the personal characteristics of effective leaders have a long and disappointing history. The search for leadership traits has not resulted in many consistent findings. Despite all the effort, only a few traits have been consistently identified. Effective leaders tend to have more task-related abilities, be more social, and have more motivation to be leaders than others. In addition, leaders'cross-cultural knowledge improves team performance in culturally diverse teams. Also, leaders who form one-to-one relationships with team members increase team performance and productivity.

While these findings indicate that a few personal characteristics do influence leadership capabilities, it is important to note that task-related abilities vary in different situations. The same is true of the kinds of social skills required of leaders in different situations. As a result, the same individual will not necessarily be an effective leader in every context.

An effective leader of an engineering product development team, for example, might be ineffective as a leader of a group in the financial or hotel industry. This leader's knowledge of the tasks of a group in another industry would, in all likelihood, be lacking. Although this may seem self-evident, in large organizations composed of many different businesses, people are often transferred among businesses without regard to task competence. Such transfers are based on the assumptions that effective leaders will be effective in a variety of contexts and that knowledge of a group's task is not essential for leadership. Research suggests that this is not the case. To be effective, leaders must understand the work of a group in depth.

The social skills required in different leadership roles also vary. An outgoing, engaging, and charming style might be required in some situations. In others, a more sedate, low-key style works best. While some people may be able to adjust their styles to meet different social demands, others may not be as successful. All leaders must adjust their styles at different times to facilitate group progress. However, leaders should be aware that certain personality characteristics are difficult to alter and task competence in very different areas is hard to come by. The bottom line, then, is that it is best to be selective about the leadership roles you take on. Choose to take on a leadership role when you understand the group's work and you believe you will be able to meet group needs.

Adjust your leadership style to meet the developmental needs of the group at a particular point in time.

Member perceptions of the role of the leader change at different stages of group development. In Stage 1, the group perceives the leader as benevolent and powerful. He or she is perceived as the source of member safety and reward. In Stage 2, members begin to challenge the leader's authority and control. For the group to mature, such challenges are necessary. The role of the leader must be redefined if the group is to move into the more mature stages of development. When power is redistributed as groups mature, all group leaders experience some loss of influence and prominence.

Groups that successfully move through the developmental sequence do so, in part, by changing the relationship between members and the leader. The leader—once benevolent, then authoritarian in the eyes of members—emerges in later stages as a more realistic group facilitator and coordinator. Earlier mythic qualities ascribed to the leader by members are stripped away, and a human being with a job to do emerges. Leader prominence is less necessary in later stages of development because goals and roles have become clear. Members' roles have emerged that take over certain aspects of the leader's role. The elaborated group social structure makes leader prominence unnecessary and potentially disruptive. Leadership is still necessary for coordination; however, both leaders and members provide that coordination.

These changes in status and perceptions take their toll on the bravest of leaders. Because most people who assume a leadership role are not aware of these naturally occurring group processes, they may feel defeated as a result of the attacks and challenges to their authority that occur in Stage 2. However, for the group to develop further, the leader's role must be significantly altered.

In mature and productive teams, members assume many of the functions leaders performed at earlier stages. For this to occur, the leader's role must become less directive and more consultative. Leaders can help to redistribute power among members by altering their leadership style to match the needs of the group. This requires knowing what the needs of the group are at any given time and how to behave to facilitate movement.

In a way, leadership and parenting have a lot in common. An effective parent interacts differently with a small child than with that same child as an adolescent or a young adult. Maintaining one parenting style throughout the life of a child would be disastrous. Maintaining one style of leadership throughout the life of a group would be detrimental as well. One style will not meet group needs and will not facilitate the development of an effective and productive team. The question for leaders, then, is, "What leadership style is best at the different stages of group development?" The following guidelines suggest ways for leaders to behave when groups are in the different stages of group development.

Leadership at Stage 1: Be a directive and confident leader.

In a new group, members expect leaders to be directive, confident, organized, and task oriented. Group members have not had the time to organize themselves yet. That will come later. In the meantime, members want the leader to provide that structure for them. Don't be afraid to do that. Many new leaders feel it best to ask members to help structure the group from the beginning. While this may seem democratic and right, it tends to make members feel insecure and slows group progress.

Come into meetings with a clear, written agenda. State the group's goals as clearly as possible. Run meetings efficiently and assign tasks to individuals as necessary. If decisions are called for, make them. Your initial attempts to organize things will be modified later as group members become more involved. In the beginning, however, providing direction and appearing confident of group success are essential.

- **Work to reduce members' anxiety, fears of rejection, and concerns about safety.**

In the first stage of group development, member dependency, anxiety, and need for inclusion and safety are at their height. The leader is likely to be seen as benevolent, competent, and the provider of safety to anxious group members. One of the leader's main jobs during this time is to reduce the anxieties of group members. Leaders can ease member anxiety by expressing confidence and providing direction. In addition, it is important to be fair and sensitive when dealing with members. Make sure you don't put individuals on the spot or react negatively to anyone. Also, help members to feel included by addressing people by name and inviting them to participate. Initially, encouraging participation is helpful. Insisting on participation or singling out nonparticipators, however, is not helpful.

- **Provide positive feedback.**

At the beginning of a group, positive feedback from the leader increases cohesion. Using your leadership position to reward rather than punish members, then, will facilitate group development. There are many ways to accomplish this. Thanking people for their attendance, input, and ideas is just one of the ways to provide positive feedback.

- **Facilitate open discussion of goals, values, and tasks.**

In the first stage of group development, leaders play an important role in facilitating group growth. This is so because leaders have the most clearly defined role during this period. Since development is progressive, the task of a leader at Stage 1 is to facilitate movement to the next developmental phase.

That is, the leader's task is to act in ways that will precipitate open discussion of values, goals, tasks, and leadership so that differences of opinion regarding these elements of group life can surface. This will move the group in the direction of Stage 2. Since people are hesitant to express different opinions at Stage 1, it is sometimes useful to ask people to express their views anonymously. This can be accomplished by asking people to write down their views on a specific issue. Next, those views can be summarized and shared with all members. This makes open discussion of divergent opinions much easier because no individual has to claim responsibility for expressing a difference of opinion or for being the first to disagree with a particular view.

- **Help members feel competent by providing supervision, training, and education in task- and process-related activities.**

It is important for members to feel competent in relation to group goals and tasks. In some groups, members enter the group with considerable skill. However, skill levels may not be the same for all group members. It's helpful to review the skills necessary to accomplish the group's tasks with all members to ensure everyone is on the same page.

Training in group participation skills is as important as training in task-related skills. Typically, group leaders have received much more training about groups than members have. As I stated earlier, hundreds of thousands of people have attended leadership training. I know of very few membership training seminars except those that I conduct myself. The assumption seems to be that if leaders understand how groups operate, they will be able to make those groups and their members behave effectively. This is not the case. Members are vital to group success and require the same knowledge and skills for group participation that leaders require.

If necessary skills either in the task or in group participation are lacking, then training, education, supervision, or a combination of these may be required to ensure group success. Again, members are unlikely to ask for these at such an early stage of development. Therefore, it is incumbent on leaders to determine what members' skill levels are and which skills might need strengthening. Anonymous surveys or private interviews with group members may be helpful in this regard. Use the Effective Member Checklist in Chapter 8 to determine what group members need to learn. It would be helpful to ask members to read this book. They will learn not only about their role as members but also about your role as leader. That will make a big, and positive, difference.

- **Set high performance standards and provide guidance as needed.**

Research tells us that groups with high performance standards tend to be more successful. Setting those standards from the beginning is very important. During discussions about goals, then, it is helpful not only to describe the product that the group is expected to generate but also to discuss expectations regarding the quality of that product. It is also helpful to review standards for group participation. Use the Effective Member Checklist in Chapter 8 and the Effective Leader Checklist in this chapter as ways of setting performance standards for member and leader participation.

- **Manage the external environment for the group.**

One of the important functions leaders must perform during the early stages of group development is managing the group's interaction with the rest of the organization. Later on, members will take over some aspects of this function. Initially, however, it falls to the leader to negotiate with other groups and individuals for needed resources, buffer the group from excessive external demands, and report on group progress as a way of ensuring that the group is regarded positively by the rest of the organization.

Leadership at Stage 2: When members begin to demand more participation in running the group, slowly begin to empower them to have it.

In the first stage of group development, leaders have considerable influence. Members tend to be dependent on the leader for direction and safety. Leaders have a good deal of influence with regard to initial definition of goals and preliminary decisions about the type of group structure being established. Group members expect the leader to provide direction, safety, order, and group goals and structures. Attempts to engage members in these activities at Stage 1 would be futile.

During Stage 2, however, member expectations and reactions to the leader change quite a bit. As members become more comfortable in the group, they begin to resent what they now perceive to be undue influence on the part of the leader. The leader's competence may be challenged. Some members may feel manipulated by the leader. The safety and competence members perceived the leader to provide are questioned. Suspicion of, and challenges to, the leader's authority often begin to take place.

Not all members become disenchanted with the leader. Some remain loyal. The group may split into two factions over this issue. One faction is supportive of the leader and the other is not. These two factions often fight about their expectations of the leader and his or her performance with regard to those expectations. Some of this conflict may be due to actual leader behavior in the group. Much of the conflict, however, is about things that go beyond the role of the leader. In essence, the conflict with and about the leader is a way for the group to discuss who can have input into decisions. Roles and decision-making, power, status, and communications structures are being clarified in this process. Efforts to redistribute power begin to occur as well. These are all necessary for group progress.

During the first stage of group development, the role of leader is the most differentiated and important role. Other roles are just being assigned. The leader role is necessary to the establishment of some sense of safety and order. In effect, the role of leader and members' reactions to that role are the impetus for the emergence of other roles and structures in the group. The prominence of the leader at Stage 1 and member dependence on the leader allow for initial structures to form. Once these are in place, the group can begin to define its structure even further. A major way that the group does this is by redefining the leader's role and reducing, to some extent, the power associated with that role. This redistribution of power clears the way for other structures and roles to emerge.

So far, this seems like a reasonable and natural transition. However, leaders have used their power during Stage 1. The acquisition of power tends to make individuals want more power, not less. Thus, the redistribution of power necessary for further group development is not an easy process. When leaders are met with resistance, their efforts to exert power and influence tend to increase, not decrease.

Three types of power have been described in the literature. There is *power over*, which is associated with dominance. *Power from* is the ability to resist unwanted influence and demands. *Power to*, or *empowerment*, is the ability to act more freely through power sharing. The strategies of power over and power from tend to have negative effects on group relationships and goal achievement. Such leadership tactics often push others to attempt to take power from the leader, and conflict is the inevitable result. Leaders who employ power-to, or empowering, strategies facilitate group development since no leader can perform all the functions of leadership alone. Redistribution of power is essential to facilitating group development and productivity.

Given the previous discussion, a group is not always successful in altering its perceptions, or the leader's perceptions, of the leadership role. Also, even if the group's perceptions change, the leader may force or coerce the group into continuing to respond as it did in Stage 1. Should the group fail to alter its perceptions, it will regress to the dependency stage of group development. Should the leader and group disagree about the leader's role and be unable to resolve this controversy, a prolonged fight for power and control is likely to occur. The group will then remain in Stage 2 for an extended time. Should that happen, the group's cohesiveness, social structure, and productivity will be very adversely affected. Power struggles, fights, and the like will take precedence over goal achievement, efficiency, and productivity.

Effective leaders expect challenges to their authority and expect member demands for more participation in running the group. These leaders see those challenges and demands as a positive sign of group progress and not as threats to their authority. They respond to these challenges by slowly beginning to empower group members to participate more equally in group management functions. Effective leaders do this slowly, since it will take members some time to work out conflicts and roles with regard to group management. Giving up the reins all at once could be disruptive. A slower redistribution of power will be most effective.

- **Don't take attacks and challenges personally.**

One of the reasons why groups fail to resolve the tension and conflict inherent in this stage of group development is that leaders and members tend to personalize the experience. That is, when others challenge an individual member's views, the individual has a natural tendency to feel hurt and personally attacked. Leaders who are attacked or discounted by members also tend to perceive these as personal affronts. As a result, individuals may become defensive or combative. This escalation of tension to unmanageable levels may significantly reduce the group's chances of resolving conflict and creating a unified group culture and structure.

BOX 9.1   From Dead Birds to the Newsroom

She was the leader of specialists working to find ways to prevent birds from flying into airplane engines. She was so effective as a leader that the corporation, which had acquired many enterprises, transferred her to a position as leader of a network newsroom.

Adopting a group perspective can be very helpful to members and leaders, especially at this stage. If the events of Stage 2 are viewed from this perspective, they are understood very differently. Rather than feeling personally attacked, a leader with a group perspective can view the attack as a sign that the group is ready to define its structure further. The leader can view her or his role at this stage as a focus or catalyst for continued development. She or he doesn't feel threatened by the loss of some power or influence. Rather, the leader views this redistribution of power, roles, and tasks as essential to group productivity and goal achievement.

In like fashion, a member whose views are challenged by others can regard challenges as necessary to the establishment of shared goals and an integrated group culture and social structure. Instead of reacting defensively, the member might focus on clarifying his or her views and the views of others in an attempt to gain consensus. A group perspective makes it possible for individuals to view conflict as normal and necessary at this stage of group development.

In real situations, on numerous occasions, I have seen the positive effects of adopting a group perspective. If a group stuck in the conflict stage can adopt a group perspective, it may be able to free itself and move to higher developmental stages. The first step is learning about group development and dynamics. Simply knowing about these phenomena, however, is not enough. Leaders and members must give up blaming each other to begin resolving the conflicts. This is not easy. Even though we know intellectually that conflict, attacks, and disagreements are normal and necessary parts of group development, on an emotional level we may feel hurt or angry. Our emotions may overwhelm us and lead us to seek revenge or vindication rather than reconciliation and consensus. In many cases, group members and leaders would rather get even than succeed.

- **Act in ways that facilitate open discussion and resolution of conflicts regarding values, goals, and leadership.**

Conflict resolution increases group cohesion and trust, which makes it possible for the group to focus on strategies to achieve shared goals. In short, it moves the group in the direction of the third stage of group development. Strategies to manage conflict were discussed in the previous chapter. They are briefly outlined again here because both members and leaders have responsibility for discussion and resolution of conflicts.

Leaders and members of successful teams communicate their views clearly and explicitly. They avoid generalizations and are specific in their communication. They talk about trust and cooperation during the discussion. Leaders and members also initially respond cooperatively to others who are behaving competitively. If others continue to respond competitively, successful group leaders and members demonstrate their willingness to compete by arguing their position.

Negotiation is an important conflict resolution strategy. Seeking a mutually agreeable solution has been found to increase communication and cooperation. It also tends to reduce conflict by breaking down the problem into specific issues that can be dealt with one at a time.

When the intensity and depth of the conflict are too great to be solved by the group members themselves, seeking the aid of a third party can help. Third-party interventions should be sought only if all parties want the help and if the intensity of the conflict is high. This last-resort strategy requires willingness on the part of the group and considerable skill on the part of the third party.

Leadership at Stage 3: Involve members in the leadership of the group.

Involving members as participants in the leadership process is the hallmark of Stage 3 leadership. Since leaders cannot perform every task, delegation and power sharing are necessary and indicative of an effective leadership style at this stage.

Leader prominence is less necessary at later stages of development because goals and roles have become clear. Member roles have emerged that take over aspects of the leader's role. The elaborated group structure makes leader prominence unnecessary and potentially disruptive. The leader moves into a more consultative role with the group. Leadership is still necessary for coordination; however, that coordination function is now shared among members and the leader. The following guidelines describe what effective leaders do at Stage 3.

- **Encourage and support members' efforts to share in the leadership function of the group.**

In Stage 3, members are ready to facilitate meetings or portions of meetings. By this time, they are capable of working in subgroups to accomplish goals. Members will be giving reports about subgroup meetings and about tasks that have been accomplished between meetings. They will be involved in decision making and conflict resolution. Members also will be involved in negotiation, scanning, buffering, and group image and profile management within the larger organization. In short, members will have assumed many of the functions performed solely by the leader at earlier stages of development.

The leader is freed up to act more as a consultant to and supporter of members. The tasks of leaders and members of Stage 3 groups are the same. By this time, the power differential between leaders and followers has been reduced and participants are operating in more egalitarian ways. All participants share equal responsibility for and commitment to the group. Their shared task is to consolidate gains in trust and cohesion and to organize themselves in ways that will ensure group productivity. Leaders who support, compliment, and praise members' efforts to share in the leadership function will increase the likelihood of group success.

- **Encourage the group to make any necessary changes in the group's structure to facilitate group productivity.**

One of the primary tasks of a Stage 3 group is to assess how it is functioning and to make any adjustments that will facilitate group productivity. Leaders encourage members to do this but don't do the work for the group. Instead, they provide ways for members to identify issues that may impede productivity and to determine ways to remove them. They also participate in identifying impediments to group success and in planning strategies to overcome them. The checklists in previous chapters are one way to approach this task.

Leadership at Stage 4: Participate as an expert member of your team.

Leaders of Stage 4 teams can relax a little. Things should be going pretty smoothly. Members have taken on responsibilities and are actively pursuing group goal achievement. Leaders continue to act as consultants as needed. In general, however, they participate along with members in achieving objectives and team success.

- **Continue to monitor team processes, especially for signs of regression.**

Each time a member leaves, new tasks are added, external conditions change, or other factors shift in some significant way, team dynamics are affected. In each of these circumstances, the team will experience disruptions and adjustments will be required to regain former levels of cohesion and productivity. Awareness and discussion of this fact of team life on the part of leaders and members is essential. Leaders and members can help maintain team effectiveness by periodically assessing the team and identifying issues that need to be addressed. In this way, a team can continually monitor its functioning and make necessary adjustments. Ways to conduct these periodic assessments are described in Chapter 6.

No team or individual sustains high levels of productivity for long stretches of time. People and groups require periods of rest, relaxation, flight, "grumpiness," and fun. Unrealistic expectations of our human capacities may be one of the biggest threats to individual and team effectiveness.

- **Conduct organizational support review regularly.**

In Chapter 10, the importance of organizational support to team success will be discussed. I recommend that relevant external individuals and groups meet with the team on a regular basis to assess the adequacy of that organizational support and to plan ways to increase the level of support, if necessary. I want to encourage leaders to ensure that these reviews happen regularly throughout the life of the group. The frequency of reviews will vary from group to group, depending on the time frame allotted to the group to accomplish its work. For example, if a product development group has 18 months to accomplish its goal, I would suggest a review at the very beginning, one about three months later, and then reviews at longer intervals. Do what makes sense for your group.

Regardless of the stage of your group, be an effective group member.

Leaders must also be effective group members. Review the Effective Member Checklist in Chapter 8 to assess how well you are doing in that regard. Also, review the Effective Leader Checklist provided next to assess how well you are doing in your current leadership role.

Effective Leader Checklist

Please read the statements below. Circle the number that most accurately describes your response to the statement. Use the following key to respond to each statement.

1 = disagree strongly

2 = disagree to some extent

3 = agree to some extent

4 = agree strongly

Section I

1. I avoid taking leadership assignments for which I do not have sufficient task-related knowledge.

    1   2   3   4

2. I avoid taking leadership assignments for which I do not have the appropriate personal style.

    1   2   3   4

3. I am motivated to act as the leader of this group.

    1   2   3   4

4. I am able to adjust my leadership style to meet the developmental needs of the group at a particular point in time.

    1   2   3   4

5. I treat members sensitively and fairly.

    1   2   3   4

6. I give lots of positive feedback to the group and to individuals.

    1   2   3   4

7. I facilitate member feelings of competence by providing supervision, training, and education in task-related skills when necessary.

    1   2   3   4

(Continued)

(Continued)

8. I facilitate member feelings of competence by providing supervision, training, and education in group participation skills when necessary.

    1   2   3   4

9. I set high performance standards from the beginning.

    1   2   3   4

10. I review quality expectations early and often.

    1   2   3   4

11. I review standards for member and leader participation as well.

    1   2   3   4

12. Regardless of the group's stage of development, I follow the guidelines for effective group membership as well as the guidelines for effective leadership.

    1   2   3   4

Section I Score: _____

Section II

13. With a Stage 1 group, I am a directive and confident leader.

    1   2   3   4

14. I come to early meetings with a clear, written agenda.

    1   2   3   4

15. At early meetings, I am able to state the group's goals clearly.

    1   2   3   4

16. Especially in the beginning, I run meetings efficiently.

    1   2   3   4

17. Early on, I am comfortable assigning tasks to individuals as necessary.

    1   2   3   4

18. Early on, I am comfortable making decisions as needed.

    1   2   3   4

19. In early meetings, I work to reduce member anxiety, fears of rejection, and concerns about safety.

    1   2   3   4

20. I address members by name and make sure members know each other's names from the beginning.

    1   2   3   4

21. I try not to put individuals on the spot, especially in early meetings.

    1   2   3   4

22. I encourage participation, but I don't demand participation.

    1   2   3   4

Section II Score: _____

Section III

23. I facilitate open discussion of group goals, values, and tasks.

    1   2   3   4

24. I encourage the expression of different points of view.

    1   2   3   4

25. When members are having difficulty expressing different opinions, I use methods to elicit their opinions anonymously.

    1   2   3   4

26. When members begin to demand more participation in running the group, I slowly begin to empower them to do so.

    1   2   3   4

27. I expect challenges to my authority and see them as a sign of group progress.

    1   2   3   4

28. I try not to take attacks and challenges personally.

    1   2   3   4

29. I facilitate open discussion and resolution of conflicts that emerge.

    1   2   3   4

30. I encourage the use of effective conflict resolution strategies.

    1   2   3   4

Section III Score: _____

(Continued)

(Continued)

Section IV

31. As the group matures, I increasingly involve members in the leadership function of the group.

        1   2   3   4

32. As the group matures, I encourage and support member efforts to share in the leadership function of the group.

        1   2   3   4

33. As the group matures, I encourage the group to make any necessary changes in the group's structure to facilitate group productivity.

        1   2   3   4

34. When a team is fully functional, I act more as an expert member than as a leader.

        1   2   3   4

35. When a team is fully functional, I continue to monitor team processes, especially for signs of regression.

        1   2   3   4

Section IV Score: _____

Section V

36. Initially, I negotiate with external groups and individuals for needed resources.

        1   2   3   4

37. Initially, I buffer the group from excessive external demands.

        1   2   3   4

38. I scan the rest of the organization to collect information that might be useful to the group.

        1   2   3   4

39. I report group progress to others to ensure that the rest of the organization has a positive image of the group.

          1   2   3   4

40. I ask the organization to review its level of support for the team on a regular basis.

          1   2   3   4

Section V Score: _____

Total Minimum Score: 40

Total Maximum Score: 160

My Score: _____

What Is Your Overall Leadership Quotient?

Total Score	Your Leadership Grade
144+	A
128–143	B
112–127	C

What Are Your Section Scores?

Section I: General Leadership Attitudes and Skills

Total Score	Your Grade
47+	A
42–46	B
36–41	C

(Continued)

(Continued)

Section II: Stage 1 Leadership

Total Score	Your Grade
36+	A
32–35	B
28–31	C

Section III: Stage 2 Leadership

Total Score	Your Grade
29+	A
25–28	B
22–24	C

Section IV: Stages 3 and 4 Leadership

Total Score	Your Grade
18+	A
16–17	B
14–15	C

Section V: Intergroup Leadership

Total Score	Your Grade
18+	A
16–17	B
14–15	C

TEN

EFFECTIVE ORGANIZATIONAL SUPPORT FOR TEAMS

———•◆•———

S ome organizations have been very successful in making the shift to a team environment. Others have not done so well. There is a compelling reason for organizations to help work groups become effective, however. Based on my assessments of over 700 work groups whose members had been working together for six months or more, only 46% of those groups were capable of contributing to their organization's goals; 54% were not. Of the 700 work groups, only 17% were high performance teams. While organizational support is not the only thing work groups need, it plays a key role.

This chapter outlines what research and theory teach us about the role of the organization in facilitating or inhibiting the development of high performance work teams. That role is quite large and very important, but it receives little organizational attention. The reason for this is simple: It is easier to create work groups and focus on group results than to address organizational issues that may be inhibiting group performance. If organizations want effective teams, however, all organization members, especially upper management, should consider using the following guidelines to create them.

Plant groups in a favorable organizational climate.

Work groups and teams function better in an organizational culture that encourages high performance by following these principles:

- Clearly define the organization's mission
- Support innovation

- Expect success
- Value superior quality and service
- Pay attention to detail
- Value team recommendations
- Set clear expectations for group output, quality, timing, and pacing
- Reward teamwork rather than individual performance

I discuss each of these principles in more detail below.

- **Clearly define the organization's mission.**

Groups flourish when their members are clear about what business they are in. This may seem obvious, but it is not always so. Once I asked a group what the mission of its organization was and the members didn't know, even though the organization's mission statement was clearly displayed on the wall of the group's meeting room. In another case, I asked a group what its organization's mission was and the members sang the mission statement! Their singing was not sweet or lyrical, but done in that singsong way that expresses derision and disrespect. Organization members not only need to know the words contained in the mission statement, but they also need to understand and believe those words.

- **Support innovation.**

Some organizations tend to do things the way they've always been done. In organizations where this is the case, or organization members believe it is the case, groups will have more difficulty being successful. When you put people together as a group, combining their intelligence and creativity, it often leads members to come up with new and unexpected ideas and solutions. If the group is functioning in an organization that encourages new ideas and new ways of doing things, group members feel energized and supported. If not, group members quickly become dispirited and begin to believe there is no point to making suggestions that challenge the status quo.

- **Expect success.**

Some organizations don't expect to be successful. This may sound absurd, but there are many examples of this attitude expressed in different ways by organization members. Here are just a few:

"What do you expect? This is a government agency."

"The CEO is leaving soon and doesn't really care about what we do."

"We're going to be merged anyway."

"People would rather be safe than successful."

If attitudes such as these exist in an organizational culture, group members won't give their best effort because they believe giving 100% is not encouraged or valued.

- **Value superior quality and service.**

In the real world, there is always some tension among quality, service, and profit. However, if organization members perceive that profit is more important than quality and service, they will become dispirited and cynical. Some examples of how this gets expressed are listed below:

"People care more about their stock options than doing a good job."

"They want us to pretend to be working to keep the inspectors off our backs."

"They talk about customer service, but they don't really mean it."

- **Pay attention to detail.**

"Get a group together and work out this policy issue" is an example of a directive from upper management that has no detail and leaves the group leader with little to go on. The alternative would be for management to give the group leader a clear definition of the group's task; all backup materials; and awareness and preplanning about group membership, time lines, meeting times, workloads, availability of potential members, and the like.

- **Value team recommendations.**

If group members believe that whatever they come up with will be rejected or changed by upper management, the chances of group success are considerably diminished. If group leaders are told in advance what the group should come up with, success is even more unlikely. Again, this is self-evident, but, unfortunately, examples such as these are all too common. In an environment where team recommendations are not valued, it is clear to all that groups are used to make the organization seem to be seeking group input when, in fact, it is not.

- **Set clear expectations for group output, quality, timing, and pacing.**

If the group is given realistic guidelines and goals for what members are expected to produce and by when, the chances of success are greatly increased. For example, it is unrealistic to give a group two months to complete a complex task, especially if the members of that group have not worked together as a group in the past. It is also unrealistic to give a group a long-term project without some way of measuring progress along the way.

- **Reward teamwork rather than individual performance.**

How to reward teamwork rather than individual performance is one of the most difficult issues organizations face with regard to setting up work groups. Most compensation systems are designed to evaluate and reward individual contributions, not team contributions. If individuals are to be motivated to work to create a high performance team, however, then the team's performance should be a determinant of compensation and bonuses.

Team compensation systems are discussed and written about quite a lot. However, most organizations still don't have team compensation systems in place. When the earlier editions of *Creating Effective Teams* were published, few team compensation systems were available. This is no longer the case. Despite the availability of these models, however, many organizations still haven't made the shift to team compensation.

Some organizations use recognition of team performance as a substitute for financial reward. Although this is helpful in some cases, this type of recognition has to be carefully thought out. Sometimes recognition of one team may create competition among teams. This can inhibit performance, because most teams rely on cooperation from other teams to accomplish their goals. In other cases, this kind of recognition can be a source of embarrassment to some team members.

Successful team compensation strategies are now readily available. Compensating employees for meeting their individual goals and for membership on a team that has met its goals and objectives is the right combination. Organizations that don't have this combination won't get maximum results from their teams.

Give groups what they need to do their best.

Work groups function better in organizations that:

- Establish meaningful group goals and tasks that involve skill, have variety, and require interdependence
- Establish meaningful group goals and tasks that require continuous learning
- Establish access to the human resources necessary to accomplish group goals
- Establish access to the technical resources necessary to accomplish tasks
- Establish defined team work areas

- **Establish meaningful group goals and meaningful tasks that involve skill, have variety, and require interdependence.**

Group members function better when they feel group goals and tasks are meaningful, interest them, and challenge them to think and work to capacity. If tasks are seen as routine or boring, motivation is diminished. Of course, many organizational tasks are routine or boring but still must be done. A team format may not be the best way to accomplish those tasks.

Group goals and tasks should also require interdependence. That is, a team should be necessary to accomplish them. Again, this seems self-evident, but a few examples will make it obvious that many groups have goals and tasks that don't require members to work together. These groups are treated as teams but in fact are not teams. Examples include:

- Phone solicitors who work independently but are called a team and meet once a week to discuss team performance
- Salespeople who work independently, are paid for individual sales, and meet once a month to discuss team performance
- The top 50 administrators in an organization, who meet monthly to hear a report from the CEO
- People who report to the same boss but don't interact with each other at any other time

- **Establish meaningful group goals and tasks that require continuous learning.**

Groups with goals and tasks that require continuous learning are the most successful groups. In fact, the best thing about a group with such goals and tasks is that its members will learn from each other and will seek out information to learn more about how to proceed. If a group's goals and tasks don't require new learning, a group format is probably not necessary for their accomplishment. Give group members the tools they need to be successful.

- **Establish access to the human resources necessary to accomplish group goals.**

A group that is expected to produce a new product on time and under budget but with no authority over or access to the people who set production schedules will not be successful. A group that is expected to determine best practices in a certain area but has no budget to visit other organizations or to consult experts in the area will, in all likelihood, be unsuccessful. A group that is mired in conflict and can't ask for assistance from an internal or external consultant to help members work out their differences also will have great difficulty being successful. Make sure team members have the help they need.

- **Establish access to the technical resources necessary to accomplish tasks.**

You can't build a house without tools. Yet many teams I've worked with were expected to accomplish tasks without even minimal access to computer equipment, fax machines, computer programs, archival materials, and other resources necessary for goal achievement.

BOX 10.1   Old English

The boss asked, "What will you guys need to do your best work?" A team member replied, "A work space with more modern equipment than Dickens used would be helpful."

- **Establish defined team work areas.**

A group needs a territory. This had been difficult for larger organizations whose group members are spread out over large geographic areas. In the earlier editions of *Creating Effective Teams*, I said that "while e-mail and teleconferencing can help to some extent, groups do better when they have regular face-to-face meetings." I have softened my opinion on that in the last few years. We have become used to conference calls, videoconferencing, Skype, and group discussions via email. Some research in this area suggests that these forms of work group interaction can function very well. I still do advocate periodic face-to-face meetings. If distance prohibits frequent meetings, those meetings should be long enough to allow for extended planning, discussions, and decision making. For groups in the same geographic location, a defined work area is very useful. Proximity makes communication easier, and the work progresses faster. We are, after all, still human. We need to know the people in our groups. We don't need to know other members intimately, but we do need to know people's thoughts and attitudes about the work we are doing together.

Pick members based on their ability to do the task and their ability to contribute to group success.

There's a lot more research about leaders than there is about members. Thousands of studies have been done to determine what makes a good group leader. Even with all the attention paid to leadership, we still don't know very much. In the case of members, we know even less.

What is known about effective members was discussed in more detail in Chapter 8. As a reminder, I can say that the research literature does not conclude that either personality assessment of potential group members or the personality or style compatibility of group members is key to group success. Rather, it suggests that work group members who are knowledgeable about how groups operate and about the group's tasks compose the best groups.

In addition, the research literature does not suggest that group members have to like each other or socialize outside of work for their groups to be successful. Instead, it suggests that people trained in the technical aspects of the job, in how groups function, and in what members and leaders can do to help the group function more effectively make good group members.

Educate people for group participation competence.

Organizations that focus on educating and training people about the technical aspects of their jobs and about effective group participation will increase the likelihood that their groups will become high performance teams.

Most organizations do a reasonable job of choosing people with technical expertise and providing ongoing technical training to their employees. When it comes to facilitating the group participation of members or leaders, however, organizations don't do so well. Most employees in large organizations have attended the obligatory half-day workshop on group dynamics, and many have attended leadership training or team development workshops. However, the quality and duration of these experiences vary widely.

Imagine providing inaccurate or incomplete computer training. Imagine giving technicians inexact information about turbine maintenance. While I'm sure that this happens occasionally, organizations tend to be careful and conservative about technical training. Unfortunately, this is not the case with group or leadership training.

BOX 10.2   Looking Good

As part of a class assignment, some of my students surveyed companies, asking how they selected outside trainers to conduct team-building workshops. The most frequent response was that the trainer's brochure and materials (projector, manuals, etc.) had to be of the highest professional quality. The trainer's references were rarely checked.

Organizations forget to ask training providers some very basic and important questions. These questions include the following:

1. What is taught in this training?

2. Is the content of the training based on solid research evidence?

3. Can the trainer provide us with social science references that support the training content?

4. Does the training work? Do people who attend this training actually perform better as group members or leaders?

These questions don't have easy answers, and training providers shouldn't be expected to answer each question completely. All training providers should be able to answer the first three pretty well, however. Trainers should be aware of the body of literature that supports the content of the training they provide. Trainers should also be aware of literature that disagrees with their approach. If a trainer is unable to answer the first three questions above, head for the hills.

With regard to the fourth question, we know that most approaches to team-building training have little or no effect. People who attend group dynamics or leadership training don't necessarily perform better as group members or leaders. This is because individuals rather than work groups are trained. More effective approaches are described in the next section.

Avoid unsubstantiated team development and consultation strategies.

Since not all work groups manage to reach high levels of effectiveness and productivity on their own, efforts to develop intervention strategies that will assist groups in meeting goals and maximizing effectiveness have been employed for many years. Unfortunately, most team interventions don't work. Sundstrom, DeMeuse, and Futrell, for example, examined a number of interventions studies and noted that four of the nine interventions had positive effects on group performance. This means that for five of the nine, performance was unchanged. At best, interventions have had mixed results on group effectiveness and productivity.

Guzzo, Jett, and Katzell conducted an analysis of 330 group intervention studies. They found that interventions that included goal setting and feedback had the most positive effects on group productivity. Interventions that take group development into account are also useful, since groups need different types of interventions at different points in their development.

To date, the most promising intervention type appears to be goal setting combined with feedback that includes attention to group development issues. The likely reason for the effectiveness of this combined intervention type is that group members set the goals and determine the strategies for improvement themselves. In short, group members and leaders are active as opposed to passive participants in the intervention process. Also, this type of intervention is tailored to meet the needs of a group at a particular point in time. It does not assume that one intervention type fits all groups.

Needless to say, research does not suggest that rock climbing, whitewater rafting, blind trust walks, or playing basketball on donkeys increases productivity in any way. These kinds of activities are fun for some people and distasteful to others. In any case, there is no evidence that they facilitate changes in group effectiveness or productivity.

Before choosing an intervention to improve group performance, organization members should ask the consultant the following questions:

1. What are the underlying assumptions of the intervention? That is, how will the intervention change the dynamics of the group?

2. Is the intervention based on solid research evidence?

3. Can the consultant provide social science references that support the intervention content?

4. Does the intervention work? Do work groups that participate in this type of intervention increase their effectiveness and productivity?

If the consultant can't answer the first three questions or bases his or her response solely on personal experience, head for the hills. Regarding the fourth question we can say that, although more research is needed, if the intervention includes goal setting, performance feedback, and attention to group development issues, it will work better than other approaches. Until we learn more, it is best to employ interventions that contain these three elements.

Avoid helping groups too much.

Many groups are getting too much help. They often have an array of helpers such as sponsors, coaches, leaders, trainers, and consultants. This help, however, is not always helpful. Throughout this chapter, I have outlined the things groups really need to function and to get moving again when they get stuck. I have found no evidence in the literature that increasing the number of expert helpers who meet with the team on a regular basis has any positive effects.

When groups ask for help, they should get that help if it conforms to the guidelines outlined here. Too much help often increases group dependency on experts and reduces the chances that group members will learn to be effective and productive on their own.

I mentioned this earlier, but I reiterate it here because it is so important: Groups need accurate and frequent feedback about their performance so that they can learn to help themselves. Without feedback, it is very difficult for groups to judge their progress or make corrections to get back on course. Some groups get lots of feedback. Others get almost none. Research tells us that groups that get feedback regularly will be more successful.

Make sure each group has enough autonomy to do its work but remains connected with the rest of the organization.

The mission of every group should be clear to other groups and individuals in the organization. If organization members and units are expected to help each other, they must know what others are doing.

Groups also need sufficient autonomy to do their work. They need to be clear about what decisions they can make on their own and what decisions need to be reviewed by others. At the same time, groups must stay in close contact with other organization members and groups. If an isolated group makes a decision without involving others in that decision, the odds of having the decision countermanded or ignored increase significantly. Groups must stay in close contact with others in the organization, as good working relationships with other organization members and groups are important indicators of an effective team.

Conduct organizational support reviews regularly.

Many of the guidelines outlined in this chapter could be read as things that only upper management can accomplish. It is not my intention to imply that. Every member of the organization has a role to play in the success of the groups with which she or he interacts. Each group has a responsibility to solicit the things necessary for its success as well.

Before and during the life of any group, it would be helpful for reviews of these guidelines to be made. Group members, or potential members, along with others external to the group who interact with the group in some meaningful way, should conduct these reviews to determine the group's level of organizational support and to make changes as needed. Periodic review sessions focused on organizational support, not group performance, will have at least two effects. First, problems with the level of organizational support can be identified and corrected early. Second, group members will be encouraged by the efforts of others to ensure that the group becomes a high performance team.

Organizational support review sessions have not been researched. However, because research has outlined a number of organizational factors that increase the chances of group success, it is only logical that organization members use such review sessions to make sure these factors are being addressed.

The checklist at the end of this chapter is provided to help people participating in an organizational support review session evaluate the level of organizational support for a particular group. Work group members should complete the checklist anonymously prior to the meeting. Ensuring individual anonymity is crucial to the success of this process. Individuals must feel free to be candid in their responses.

A summary should be prepared prior to the meeting. At the meeting, participants should discuss the summary and identify areas where organizational support is adequate or superior and areas that need improvement. Action steps should be outlined as well. Although there will be areas where, for legitimate reasons, support can't be provided at ideal levels, both the work group and the organization it belongs to should aim to do the best they can.

Good luck to all the teams out there. Individual heroism is a fine thing, but we need heroic teams as well. Any time you hear of a scientific advancement, a new medicine, or a school where student achievement has improved significantly, a heroic team was behind it.

Thanks!

The Organizational Support Checklist

Please read the statements below. Circle the number that most accurately describes your response to the statement. Use the following key to respond to each statement.

1 = disagree strongly

2 = disagree to some extent

3 = agree to some extent

4 = agree strongly

Section I

1. This organization supports innovation.

    1   2   3   4

2. This organization expects to be successful.

    1   2   3   4

3. This organization values superior quality in all work endeavors.

    1   2   3   4

4. Organization members pay attention to detail.

    1   2   3   4

5. This organization values team recommendations.

    1   2   3   4

Section I Score: _____

Section II

6. This organization has a clearly defined organizational mission.

    1   2   3   4

7. This organization has clear expectations about the quality of our group's output.

    1   2   3   4

(Continued)

(Continued)

8. This organization has clear expectations for our group's timing and deadlines.

1	2	3	4

9. Our group's goals are clear to the rest of the organization.

1	2	3	4

Section II Score: _____

Section III

10. The goals and tasks of our group are meaningful.

1	2	3	4

11. Our group's tasks are interesting to group members.

1	2	3	4

12. Our group's tasks require group members to work collaboratively.

1	2	3	4

13. Our group's tasks require continuous learning.

1	2	3	4

14. Our group has been provided with members with appropriate technical skills.

1	2	3	4

Section III Score: _____

Section IV

15. Our group has access to the technical resources necessary to accomplish its tasks.

1	2	3	4

16. Our group has access to the human resources necessary to accomplish its tasks.

1	2	3	4

17. Our group has a defined work area.

             1   2   3   4

18. Our group has sufficient autonomy to do its work.

             1   2   3   4

19. Our group is in close communication with appropriate organization members and groups.

             1   2   3   4

Section IV Score: _____

Section V

20. Our group receives regular feedback about its performance and progress.

             1   2   3   4

21. Our group receives positive recognition for group achievements.

             1   2   3   4

22. Rewards and recognition are based on group achievements.

             1   2   3   4

Section V Score: _____

Section VI

23. Our group has been provided with members with skills in the area of group participation.

             1   2   3   4

24. Our group has been provided with a leader with skills in the area of group management and participation.

             1   2   3   4

25. Our group has been provided with all technical training necessary for group success.

             1   2   3   4

(Continued)

(Continued)

---

26. Our group has been provided with appropriate team training.

    1   2   3   4

27. Our group leader has been provided with appropriate leadership training.

    1   2   3   4

28. Our group has been provided with the help of consultants when it has been deemed necessary for group success.

    1   2   3   4

Section VI Score: _____

Section VII

If group training has been provided to your group, please answer the following questions.

29. I learned what I needed to know to work successfully with this group.

    1   2   3   4

30. I felt that the trainer was competent.

    1   2   3   4

If group consultation has been provided to your group, please answer the following questions.

31. The consultation helped the group members to work more effectively together.

    1   2   3   4

32. I felt that the consultant was competent.

    1   2   3   4

Section VII Score: _____

Maximum Score: 128
Minimum Score: 32

My Score: _____

What Is the Overall Level of Organizational Support?

Total Score	Organization's Grade
115+	A
103–114	B
89–102	C

What Are the Section Scores?

Section I: Organizational Culture

Total Score	Organization's Grade
18+	A
16–17	B
14–15	C

Section II: Mission Clarity

Total Score	Organization's Grade
14+	A
12–13	B
10–11	C

Section III: Task and Technology

Total Score	Organization's Grade
18+	A
16–17	B
14–15	C

(Continued)

(Continued)

Section IV: Autonomy and Access

Total Score	Organization's Grade
14+	A
12–13	B
10–11	C

Section V: Feedback and Recognition

Total Score	Organization's Grade
11+	A
9–10	B
7–8	C

Section VI: Training and Development

Total Score	Organization's Grade
22+	A
19–21	B
16–18	C

Section VII: Training Quality

Total Score	Organization's Grade
14+	A
12–13	B
10–11	C

BIBLIOGRAPHY

———•◆•———

This bibliography has been divided into the following 10 sections: groups and group development; groups and productivity; organizational culture; effective group membership; effective leadership; diversity in work teams; effective meetings; group processes and structures; team building, organizational development, and staff development; and team compensation.

Groups and Group Development

Arrow, H., Poole, M. S., Bouas Henry, K., Wheelan, S., & Moreland, R. (2004). Time, change, and development: The temporal perspectives on groups. *Small Group Research, 35,* 73–105.

Bennis, W., & Shepard, H. (1956). A theory of group development. *Human Relations, 9,* 415–437.

Bion, W. (1961). *Experiences in groups.* New York, NY: Basic Books.

Burnand, G. (1990). Group development phases as working through six fundamental human problems. *Small Group Research, 21,* 255–273.

Caple, R. (1978). The sequential stages of group development. *Small Group Behavior, 9,* 470–476.

Devine, D. J., Clayton, L. D., Philips, J. L., Dunford, B. B., & Melner, S. B. (1999). Teams in organizations: Prevalence, characteristics, and effectiveness. *Small Group Research, 30,* 678–711.

Gordon, J. (1992). Work teams: How far have they come? *Training, 29,* 59–65.

Hogan, R. (1975). Theoretical egocentrism and the problem of compliance. *American Psychologist, 30,* 533–539.

Mills, T. (1964). *Group transformations: An analysis of a learning group.* Englewood Cliffs, NJ: Prentice Hall.

Slater, P. (1966). *Microcosm.* New York, NY: John Wiley.

Tuckman, B. W. (1965). Developmental sequence in small groups. *Psychological Bulletin, 63*(6), 384–399.

Tuckman, B. W., & Jensen, M. A. C. (1977). Stages in small group development revisited. *Group and Organizational Studies, 2,* 419–427.

Verdi, A. F., & Wheelan, S. (1992). Developmental patterns in same-sex and mixed-sex groups. *Small Group Research, 23*(3), 256–278.

Wheelan, S. (2004). Workplace teams. In J. L. DeLucia-Waack, D. A. Gerrity, C. R. Kalodner, & M. T. Riva (Eds.), *Handbook of group work* (pp. 401–413). Thousand Oaks, CA: Sage.

Wheelan, S. (2005). *Faculty groups: From frustration to collabration.* Thousand Oaks, CA: Sage.

Wheelan, S. (2005). *Group processes: A developmental perspective* (2nd ed.). Boston, MA: Allyn & Bacon.

Wheelan, S. (2005). *Handbook of group research and practice.* Thousand Oaks, CA: Sage.

Wheelan, S. (2009). Group size, group development and group productivity. *Small Group Research, 40*(2), *247–262.*

Wheelan, S. (2010). *Att skapa effektiva team.* Stockholm, Sweden: Studentlitteratur.

Wheelan, S., Davidson, B., & Tilin, F. (2003). Group development: Reality or illusion? *Small Group Research, 34,* 223–245.

Wheelan, S., & McKeage, R. (1993). Developmental patterns in small and large groups. *Small Group Research, 24*(1), 60–83.

Wheelan, S., & Verdi, A. (1992). Differences in male and female patterns of communication in groups: A methodological artifact? *Sex Roles: A Journal of Research, 27*(1/2), 1–15.

Wheelan, S., Verdi, A., & McKeage, R. (1994). *The Group Development Observation System: Origins and applications.* Philadelphia, PA: P.E.P. Press.

Wheelan, S., & Williams, T. (2003). Mapping dynamic interaction patterns in work groups. *Small Group Research, 34,* 443–467.

Groups and Productivity

Bruner, D. Y., & Greenlee, B. J. (2000). Measures of work culture in high and low performing schools. *Research in the Schools, 7*(2), 71–76.

Campany, N., Dubinsky, R., Urch Druskat, V., Mangino, M., & Flynn, E. (2007). *Organizational Development Journal, 25*(2), 179–186.

Evans, C. R., & Dion, K. L. (1991). Group cohesion and performance: A meta-analysis. *Small Group Research, 22*(2), 175–186.

Flowers, N., Mertens, S. B., & Mulhull, P. F. (1999). The impact of teaming: Five research-based outcomes. *Middle School Journal, 31*(2), 57–60.

Greene, C. N. (1989). Cohesion and productivity in work groups. *Small Group Behavior, 20,* 70–86.

Guzzo, R. A. (1990). Productivity research: Reviewing psychological and economic perspectives. In J. P. Campbell, R. J. Campbell, & Associates (Eds.), *Productivity in organizations* (pp. 63–81). San Francisco, CA: Jossey-Bass.

Hackman, J. R. (1990). *Groups that work (and those that don't).* San Francisco, CA: Jossey-Bass.

Hoy, K., & Hannum, J. W. (1997). Middle school climate: An empirical assessment of organizational health and student achievement. *Educational Administration Quarterly, 33*(3), 290–311.

Larson, C. E., & LaFasto, F. M. J. (1989). *Team work: What must go right/What can go wrong.* Newbury Park, CA: Sage.

Pritchard, R. D., Jones, S., Roth, P., Stuebing, K., & Ekeberg, S. (1988). Effects of group feedback, goal setting, and incentives on organizational productivity. *Journal of Applied Psychology, 73*(2), 337–358.

Reich, R. B. (1987). Entrepreneurship reconsidered: The team as hero. *Harvard Business Review, 64*(3), 77–83.

Shea, G. P., & Guzzo, R. A. (1987). Group effectiveness: What really matters? *Sloan Management Review, 3,* 25–31.

Shea, G. P., & Guzzo, R. A. (1987). Groups as human resources. In K. M. Rowland & G. R. Ferris (Eds.), *Research in personnel and human resources management* (Vol. 5, pp. 323–356). Greenwich, CT: JAI.

Sundstrom, E., DeMeuse, K. P., & Futrell, D. (1990). Work teams: Applications and effectiveness. *American Psychologist, 45*(2), 120–133.

Wheelan, S., & Brewer Danganan, N. (2003). The relationship between the internal dynamics of student affairs leadership teams and campus leaders' perceptions of the effectiveness of student affairs divisions. *National Association of Student Personnel Administrators Journal, 40*(3), 93–112.

Wheelan, S., & Burchill, C. (April, 1999). Take teamwork to new heights. *Nursing Management,* 28–32.

Wheelan, S., Burchill, C., & Tilin, F. (2003). The link between teamwork and patients' outcomes in intensive care units. *American Journal of Critical Care, 12,* 527–534.

Wheelan, S., & Kesselring, J. (2005). The link between faculty group development and the performance of elementary students on standardized tests. *The Journal of Educational Research, 98,* 323–330.

Wheelan, S., & Lisk, A. (2000). Cohort group effectiveness and the educational achievement of adult undergraduate students. *Small Group Research, 31*(6), 724–738.

Wheelan, S., Murphy, D., Tsumura, E., & Fried-Kline, S. (1998). Member perceptions of internal group dynamics and productivity. *Small Group Research. 29*(3), 371–393.

Wheelan, S., & Tilin, F. (1999). The relationship between faculty group effectiveness and school productivity. *Small Group Research, 30*(1), 59–81.

Wheelan, S., Tillin, F., & Sanford, J. (1996). School group effectiveness and productivity. *Research Practice, 4*(1), 11–14.

Organizational Culture

Ancona, D. G. (1987). Groups in organizations: Extending laboratory models. In C. Hendrick (Ed.), *Group and intergroup processes* (pp. 207–230). Beverly Hills, CA: Sage.

Cohen, M. D., & Sproull, L. S. (Eds.). (1996). *Organizational learning.* Thousand Oaks, CA: Sage.

Deal, T., & Peterson, K. (1999). *Shaping school culture: The heart of leadership.* San Francisco, CA: Jossey-Bass.

Deutsch, M. (1990). Forms of social organization: Psychological consequences. In H. T. Himmelweit & G. Gaskell (Eds.), *Societal psychology* (pp. 157–176). Newbury Park, CA: Sage.

Drach-Zahavy, A. (2011). Interorganizational teams as boundary spanners: The role of team diversity, boundedness, and extrateam links. *European Journal of Work and Organizational Psychology, 20*(1),71–80.

Kaifi, B., & Noori, S. (2011). Organizational behavior: A study on managers, employees, and teams. *Journal of Management Policy and Practice, 12*(2), 88–98.

Kennedy, F. A., Loughry, M. L., Klammer, T. P., & Beyerlein, M. M. (2009). Effects of organizational support on potency in work teams: The mediating role of team processes. *Small Group Research, 40*(1), 72–93.

O'Neil, J. (1995). On schools as learning organizations: A conversation with Peter Senge. *Educational Leadership, 52*(7), 20–23.

Schein, E. H. (1980). *Organizational psychology* (3rd ed.). Englewood Cliffs, NJ: Prentice Hall.

Schein, E. H. (1990). Organizational culture. *American Psychologist, 45*(2), 109–119.

Schein, E. (1991). What is culture? In P. J. Frost, L. F. Moore, M. R. Louis, C. C. Lundberg, & J. Martin (Eds.), *Reframing organizational culture* (pp. 243–253). Newbury Park, CA: Sage.

Tjosvold, D. (1991). *The conflict-positive organization: Stimulate diversity and create unity.* Reading, MA: Addison-Wesley.

Tjosvold, D., Dann, V., & Wong, C. (1992). Managing conflict between departments to serve customers. *Human Relations, 45,* 1035–1054.

Walton, R. E. (1985). From control to commitment in the workplace. *Harvard Business Review, 63*(2), 76–84.

Wheelan, S., & Abraham, M. (1993). The concept of intergroup mirroring: Reality or illusion? *Human Relations, 46*(7), 803–825.

Wheelan, S., & Conway, C. (1991). Group development as a framework to understand and promote school readiness to engage in an OD project. *The Journal of Educational and Psychological Consultation, 2*(1), 59–71.

Wheelan, S., & Krasick, C. (1993). The emergence, transmission, and acceptance of themes in a temporary organization. *Group and Organization Management, 18*(2), 237–260.

Effective Group Membership

Allen, M., & Bourhis, J. (1996). The relationship of communication apprehension to communication behavior: A meta-analysis. *Communication Quarterly, 44,* 214–226.

Bass, B. M., Wurster, C. R., Doll, P. A., & Clair, D. J. (1953). Situational and personality factors in leadership among sorority women. *Psychological Monographs, 67,* 16.

Buck, R., Miller, R. E., & Caul, W. F. (1974). Sex, personality, and physiological variables in the communication of affect via facial expression. *Journal of Personality and Social Psychology, 30,* 587–596.

Haythorn, W. (1953). The influence of individual members on the characteristics of small groups. *Journal of Abnormal and Social Psychology, 48,* 276–284.

Karau, S. J., & Williams, K. D. (1993). Social loafing: A meta-analytic review and theoretical integration. *Journal of Personality and Social Psychology, 65,* 681–706.

Kogan, N., & Wallach, M. A. (1967). Group risk taking as a function of members' anxiety and defensiveness. *Journal of Personality, 35,* 50–63.

Leonard, R. L., Jr. (1975). Self-concept and attraction for similar and dissimilar others. *Journal of Personality and Social Psychology, 31,* 926–929.

McCroskey, J. C., Hamilton, P. R., & Weiner, A. N. (1974). The effect of interaction behavior on source credibility, homophily, and interpersonal attraction. *Human Communication Research, 1,* 42–52.

Ryan, E. D., & Lakie, W. L. (1965). Competitive and noncompetitive performance in relation to achievement motive and manifest anxiety. *Journal of Personality and Social Psychology, 1,* 342–345.

Sorrentino, R. M., & Sheppard, B. H. (1978). Effects of affiliation-related motives on swimmers in individual versus group competition: A field experiment. *Journal of Personality and Social Psychology, 36,* 704–714.

Teichman, Y. (1974). Predisposition for anxiety and affiliation. *Journal of Personality and Social Psychology, 29,* 405–410.

Effective Leadership

Burke, W. W. (1986). Leadership as empowering others. In S. Srivasta & Associates (Eds.), *Executive power: How executives influence people and organizations* (pp. 51–77). San Francisco, CA: Jossey-Bass.

Cole, M., Bedeian, A., & Bruch, H. (2011). Linking leader behavior and leadership consensus to team performance. *Leadership Quarterly, 22*(2), 383–392.

Conger, T. A., & Kanugo, R. N. (1988). *Charismatic leadership: The elusive factor in organizational effectiveness.* San Francisco, CA: Jossey-Bass.

Dutton, J. E., Dukerich, J. M., & Harquail, C. V. (1994). Organizational images and member identification. *Administrative Science Quarterly, 39,* 239–263.

Hackman, J. R. (2002). *Leading teams: Setting the stage for great performances.* Boston, MA: Harvard Business School Press.

Hart, A. (1990). Managing school performance: The role of the administrator. In P. Reyes (Ed.), *Teachers and their workplace: Commitment, performance, and productivity.* Newbury Park, CA: Sage.

Haslam, S. A., McGarty, C., Brown, P. M., Eggins, R. A., Morrison, B. E., & Reynolds, K. J. (1998). Inspecting the emperor's clothes: Evidence that random selection of leaders can enhance group performance. *Group Dynamics, 2,* 168–184.

Hershey, P., & Blanchard, K. H. (1976). Leader effectiveness and adaptability description (LEAD). In J. W. Pfeiffer & J. E. Jones (Eds.), *The 1976 annual handbook for group facilitators* (Vol. 5). La Jolla, CA: University Associates.

Hershey, P., & Blanchard, K. H. (1982). *Management of organizational behavior: Utilizing human resources* (4th ed.). Englewood Cliffs, NJ: Prentice Hall.

Hollander, E. P. (1995). Organizational leadership and followership. In P. Collett & A. Furnam (Eds.), *Social psychology at work* (pp. 69–87). London, UK: Routledge.

Lumsden, G., & Lumsden, D. (1993). *Communicating in groups and teams: Sharing leadership.* Belmont, CA: Wadsworth.

Nicholls, J. R. (1985). A new approach to situational leadership. *Leadership and Organizational Development Journal, 6*(4), 2–7.

Turner, J. C., Oakes, P. J., Haslam, S. A., & McGarty, C. A. (1994). Self and collective: Cognition and social context. *Personality and Social Psychology Bulletin, 20,* 454–463.

Vecchio, R. P. (1987). Situational leadership theory: An examination of a prescriptive theory. *Journal of Applied Psychology, 72,* 444–451.

Von Cranach, M. (1986). Leadership as a function of group action. In C. F. Graumann & S. Moscovici (Eds.), *Changing conceptions of leadership* (pp. 115–134). New York, NY: Springer Verlag.

Vroom, V. H., & Jago, A. G. (1978). On the validity of the Vroom/Yetton model. *Journal of Applied Psychology, 63,* 151–162.

Vroom, V. H., & Yetton, P. W. (1973). *Leadership and decision-making.* Pittsburgh, PA: University of Pittsburgh Press.

Wheelan, S. (2003). An initial exploration of the internal dynamics of leadership teams. *Consulting Psychology Journal, 55*(3), 179–188.

Diversity in Work Teams

Brief, A. P. (2008). *Diversity at Work.* New York, NY: Cambridge University Press.

Ely, R. J., & Roberts, L. M. (2008). Shifting frames in team-diversity research: From difference to relationships. In A. Brief (Ed.), *Diversity at work* (pp. 175–201). New York, NY: Cambridge University Press.

Ely, R. J., & Thomas, D. A. (2001). Cultural diversity at work: The effects of diversity perspectives on work group processes and outcomes. *Administrative Science Quarterly, 46*(2), 229–273.

Jackson, S. E., Joshi, A., & Erhardt, N. L. (2003). Recent research on team and organizational diversity, SWOT analysis and implications. *Journal of Management, 29,* 801–830.

Jehn, K. A. (1995). A multi-method examination of the benefits and detriments of intragroup conflict. *Administrative Science Quarterly, 40,* 256–282.

Jehn, K. A., Greer, L. L., & Rupert, J. (2008). Diversity, conflict, and their consequences. In A. Brief (Ed.), *Diversity at work* (pp. 127–174). New York, NY: Cambridge University Press.

Kirchler, E., & Davis, J. H. (1986). The influence of member status differences and task type on group consensus and member position change. *Journal of Personality and Social Psychology, 51,* 83–91.

Lockheed, E., & Hall, K. (1976). Conceptualizing sex as a status characteristic: Applications to leadership training strategies. *Journal of Social Issues, 32,* 111–124.

Mannix, E. A., & Neale, M. A. (2005). What differences make a difference? The promise and reality of diverse teams in organizations. *Psychological Science in the Public Interest, 6*(2), 32–55.

Page, S. E. (2007). *The difference.* Princeton, NJ: Princeton University Press.

Roberge, M.-E., & van Dick, R. (2010). Recognizing the benefits of diversity: When and how does diversity increase group performance? *Human Resource Management, 20*(4), 295.

van der Zee, K., Vos, M., & Luijters, K. (2009). Social identity and trust in demographically diverse work teams. *Social Science Information, 48*(2), 175.

Wheelan, S. (1996). Effects of gender composition and group status differences on member perceptions of group developmental patterns, effectiveness, and productivity. *Sex Roles, 34*(9/10), 665–686.

Effective Meetings

Poole, M. S. (1991). Procedures for managing meetings: Social and technological innovation. In R. A. Swanson & B. O. Knapp (Eds.), *Innovative meeting management* (pp. 53–110). Austin, TX: 3M Meeting Management Institute.

Shelton, M. M., & Bauer, L. K. (1994). *Secrets of highly effective meetings.* Thousand Oaks, CA: Corwin.

Silberman, S. (1999). *101 ways to make meetings active: Surefire ideas to engage your group.* New York, NY: John Wiley.

Tropman, J. E. (2003). *Making meetings work: Achieving high quality group decisions.* Thousand Oaks, CA: Corwin.

Group Processes and Structures

Amason, A. C., & Schweiger, D. M. (1994). Resolving the paradox of conflict, strategic decision making, and organizational performance. *International Journal of Conflict Management, 5,* 239–253.

Argote, L., Gruenfeld, D., & Naquin, C. (2001). Group learning in organizations. In M. E. Turner (Ed.), *Groups at work: Advances in theory and research* (pp. 369–411). Mahwah, NJ: Lawrence Erlbaum.

Barr, S. H., & Conlon, E. J. (1994). Effects of distribution of feedback in work groups. *Academy of Management Journal, 37*(3), 641–655.

Bunderson, J. S., & Sutcliffe, K. (2002). Comparing alternative conceptualizations of functional diversity in management teams: Process and performance effects. *Academy of Management Journal, 45,* 875–893.

Carnevale, P. J. D. (1986). Mediating disputes and decisions in organizations. In R. J. Lewicki, B. H. Sheppard, & M. H. Bazerman (Eds.), *Research on negotiation in organizations* (Vol. 1, pp. 251–269). Greenwich, CT: JAI.

Deutsch, M. (1971). Toward an understanding of conflict. *International Journal of Group Tensions, 1,* 42–54.

Deutsch, M. (1990). Cooperation, conflict, and justice. In S. Wheelan, E. Pepitone, & V. Abt (Eds.), *Advances in field theory* (pp. 149–164). Newbury Park, CA: Sage.

Fisher, C. D., & Gitelson, R. (1983). A meta-analysis of the correlates of role conflict and ambiguity. *Journal of Applied Psychology, 68,* 320–333.

Gabarro, J. J. (1987). The development of working relationships. In J. W. Lorsch (Ed.), *Handbook of organizational behavior* (pp.172–189). Englewood Cliffs, NJ: Prentice Hall.

Glynn, M. A., & Barr, P. S. (2003). Team decision making in organizations. In M. A. West, D. Tjosvold, & K. G. Smith (Eds.), *International handbook of organizational teamwork and cooperative learning* (pp. 211–228). New York, NY: John Wiley.

Gratwitch, M. J., Munz, D. C., Elliott, E. K., & Mathis, A. (2003). Promoting creativity in temporary problem-solving groups: The effects of positive mood and autonomy in problem definition on idea-generating performance. *Group Dynamics, 7,* 200–213.

Hembroff, L. A. (1982). Resolving status inconsistency: An expectation states theory and test. *Social Forces, 61,* 183–205.

Hembroff, L. A., & Myers, D. E. (1984). Status characteristics: Degrees of task relevance and decision process. *Social Psychology Quarterly, 47,* 337–346.

Kemery, E. R., Bedeian, A. G., Mossholder, K. W., & Touliatos, J. (1985). Outcomes of role stress: A multisample constructive replication. *Academy of Management Review, 28,* 103–110.

Keyton, J. (1999). Relational communication in groups. In L. R. Frey, D. S. Gouran, & M. S. Poole (Eds.), *The handbook of group communication theory and research* (pp. 251–287). Thousand Oaks, CA: Sage.

Lovelace, K., Shapiro, D., & Weingart, L. R. (2001). Maximizing cross-functional new product teams' innovativeness and constraint adherence: A conflict communications perspective. *Academy of Management Journal, 24,* 779–784.

Miller, C. E., Jackson, P., Mueller, J., & Schersching, C. (1987). Some social psychological effects of group decision rules. *Journal of Personality and Social Psychology, 52,* 325–332.

Miller, C. E., & Wong, J. (1986). Coalition behavior: Effects of earned versus unearned resources. *Organizational Behavior and Human Decision Processes, 38,* 257–277.

Morris, W. N., & Miller, R. S. (1975). The effects of consensus-breaking and consensus pre-empting partners on reduction of conformity. *Journal of Experimental Social Psychology, 11,* 215–223.

Moscovici, S. (1985). Innovation and minority influence. In S. Moscovici, G. Mugny, & E. V. Avermate (Eds.), *Perspectives on minority influence* (pp. 9–48). Cambridge, UK: Cambridge University Press.

Moscovici, S. (1985). Social influence and conformity. In G. Lindzey & E. Aronson (Eds.), *Handbook of social psychology* (3rd ed., Vol. 1, pp. 347–412). New York, NY: Random House.

Nadler, D. A. (1979). The effects of feedback on task group behaviors: A review of the experimental research. *Organizational Behavior and Human Performance, 23,* 309–338.

Nadler, D. A., Cammann, C. T., & Mirvis, P. H. (1980). Developing a feedback system for work units: Field experiment in structural change. *Journal of Applied Behavioral Science, 16*(1), 41–62.

Peele, H. E. (2006). Appreciative inquiry and creative problem solving in cross-functional teams. *Journal of Applied Behavioral Science, 42*(4), 447–467.

Pruitt, D. G. (1987). Creative approaches to negotiation. In D. J. D. Sandole & I. Sandole-Staroste (Eds.), *Conflict management and problem solving: Interpersonal to international applications* (pp. 62–76). London, UK: Frances Pinter.

Pruitt, D. G., & Carnevale, P. J. D. (1992). The development of integrative agreements. In V. J. Derlega & J. Grezlak (Eds.), *Cooperative and helping behavior* (pp. 151–181). New York, NY: Academic Press.

Rawlins, W. K. (1984). Consensus in decision-making groups: A conceptual history. In G. M. Phillips & J. T. Wood (Eds.), *Emergent issues in human decision-making* (pp. 19–39). Carbondale: Southern Illinois University Press.

Salazar, A. J., Hirokawa, R. Y., Propp, K. M., Julian, K. M., & Leatham, G. B. (1994). In search of true causes: Examination of the effect of group potential and group interaction on decision performance. *Human Communication Research, 20,* 529–559.

Stewart, G. L. (2006). A meta-analytic review of relationships between team design features and team performance. *Journal of Management, 32*(1), 29–54.

Sundstrom, E., & Altman, I. (1989). Physical environments and work group effectiveness. In L. L. Cummings & B. Staw (Eds.), *Research in organizational behavior* (Vol. 11, pp. 175–209).

Theodorson, G. A. (1962). The function of hostility in small groups. *Journal of Social Psychology, 256,* 57–66.

Weldon, E., Jehn, K., & Pradhan, P. (1991). Processes that mediate the relationship between a group goal and improved group performance. *Journal of Personality and Social Psychology, 61*(4), 555–569.

Wheelan, S. (2009). Group size, group development, and group productivity. *Small Group Research, 40*(2), 247–262.

Team Building, Organizational Development, and Staff Development

Buzaglo, G., & Wheelan, S. (1999). Facilitating work team effectiveness: Case studies from Central America. *Small Group Research, 30,* 108–129.

Cummings, T. G. (1981). Designing effective work groups. In P. C. Nystrom & W. Starbuck (Eds.), *Handbook of organizational design* (Vol. 2, pp. 250–271). Oxford, UK: Oxford University Press.

Evans, N., & Jarvis, D. (1986). The group attitude scale: A measure of attraction to group. *Small Group Behavior, 17*(2), 203–216.

Goldstein, I. L. (Ed.). (1989). *Training and development in organizations.* San Francisco, CA: Jossey-Bass.

Guskey, T. R. (1988). Teacher efficacy, self-concept, and attitudes toward the implication of instructional innovation. *Teacher and Teacher Education, 4,* 63–69.

Guzzo, R. A., Jett, R. D., & Katzell, R. A. (1985). The effects of psychologically-based intervention programs on worker productivity: A meta-analysis. *Personnel Psychology, 38,* 275–291.

Joyce, B., & Showers, B. (1995). *Student achievement through staff development: Fundamentals of school renewal* (2nd ed.). New York, NY: Longman.

Salas, E., Rozell, D., Mullen, B., & Driskell, J. E. (1999). The effect of team building on performance: An integration. *Small Group Research, 30,* 309–329.

Schein, E. H. (1988). *Process consultation* (Rev. ed.). Reading, MA: Addison-Wesley.

Silberman, M. (1990). *Active training.* Lexington, MA: Lexington Books.

Tannenbaum, S. I., Beard, R. L., & Salas, E. (1992). Team building and its influence on team effectiveness: An examination of conceptual and empirical developments. In K. Kelley (Ed.), *Issues, theory, and research in industrial/organizational psychology.* Amsterdam, Netherlands: Elsevier.

Wheelan, S. (1990). *Facilitating training groups.* New York, NY: Praeger.

Wheelan, S., Brunner, A., Burchill, C., Craig, R., & Tilin, F. (1996). The utility of group development theory in consulting with small, social service organizations: A case study. *Organization Development Journal, 14*(3), 4–15.

Wheelan, S., Buzaglo, G., & Tsumura, E. (1998). Developing assessment tools for cross cultural group research. *Small Group Research, 29*(3), 359–370.

Wheelan, S., & Furber, S. (2006). Facilitating team development: Communication and productivity. In L. Frey (Ed.), *Facilitating group communication in context: Innovations and applications with natural groups* (Vol. 2, pp. 155–176). Thousand Oaks, CA: Sage.

Wheelan, S., & Hochberger, J. (1996). Validation studies of the Group Development Questionnaire. *Small Group Research, 27*(1), 143–170.

Team Compensation

Brown, M., & Heywood, J. S. (2002). *Paying for performance: An international comparison.* London, UK: M. E. Sharpe.

Caudron, S. (1994). Tie individual pay to team success. *Personnel Journal, 73*(19), 40–46.

Fehr, E., & Falk, A. (2002). Psychological foundations of incentives. *European Economic Review, 14,* 687–724.

Gross, S. E. (1995). *Compensation for teams: How to design and implement team-based reward systems.* New York, NY: American Management Association.

Hamilton, B., Nickerson, J., & Owan, H. (2003). Team incentives and worker heterogeneity: An empirical analysis of the impact of teams on productivity and participation. *Journal of Political Economy, 111,* 465–497.

Honeywell, J. A., Dickinson, A. M., & Poling, A. (1997). Individual performance as a function of individual and group pay contingencies. *Psychological Record, 47*(2), 261–274.

Kauhanen, A., & Piekkola, H. (2006). What makes performance-related pay schemes work? Finnish evidence. *Journal of Management Governance, 10,* 149–177.

Mohrman, S. A., Cohen, S. G., & Mohrman, A. M., Jr. (1995). *Designing team-based organizations: New forms of knowledge work.* San Francisco, CA: Jossey-Bass.

Parker, G., McAdams, J., & Zielinski, D. (2000). *Rewarding teams: Lessons from the trenches.* San Francisco, CA: Jossey-Bass.

Saunier, A. M., & Hawk, E. J. (1994). Realizing the potential of teams through team-based rewards. *Compensation and Benefits Review, 26*(4), 24–33.

Sherriton, J., & Stern, J. (1997). *Corporate culture/team culture: Removing the hidden barriers to team success.* New York, NY: American Management Association.

Zingheim, P. K., & Schuster, J. R. (1997). Best practices for small-team pay. *ACA Journal, 6*(1), 40–49.

INDEX

ABOUT THE AUTHOR

Susan Wheelan is president of GDQ Associates, Inc. Until 2001, she was professor of psychological studies and faculty director of the Training and Development Center at Temple University. Dr. Wheelan received Temple University's Great Teacher Award in 1992. She has also worked as a psychologist in a number of hospital and clinical settings. Currently, Dr. Wheelan is engaged in a number of research projects and consults with work groups in the U.S. and Europe.

Dr. Wheelan is author of *Facilitating Training Groups*; *Group Processes: A Developmental Perspective*; *Creating Effective Teams: A Guide for Members and Leaders*; and *Faculty Groups: From Frustration to Collaboration*. She is editor of the *Handbook of Group Research and Practice* and co-editor of *The Lewin Legacy: Field Theory in Current Practice and Advances in Field Theory*. She has also written numerous research articles for publication.